SNOWSHILL

A GLOUCESTERSHIRE VILLAGE

CAROLYN MASON

Published by
THORNHILL PRESS
24 Moorend Road
Cheltenham
Glos.
MCMLXXXVII

ISBN 0 946328 16 1

Printed by
Stoate & Bishop (Printers) Ltd.,
Gloucester and Cheltenham

Contents

Cover photograph (by the Author)
Snowshill Manor Cottages 1986

Acknowledgements

I am indebted to the people of Snowshill who have given me so much help and encouragement in the writing of this history. These include Mrs. Susan Byrd, Mrs. Eileen Edgworth, Mr. Frank Gunn, Mrs. Nancy Haines, Mrs. Eila Harrison, Mr. Jack Hodge, Mr. and Mrs. 'Nurk' Meadows, Mr. Hans Schad and Mrs. Sheila Wilkes who kindly allowed me to reproduce old photographs in her possession.

I am also most grateful to Mr. John Bourne and Mr. Christopher Bourne of Snowshill Hill and Mr. Michael Jessup, administrator of Snowshill Manor, for permission to study documents.

I am deeply indebted to the National Trust both here in Snowshill and at the Severn Regional Office in Tewkesbury for their very considerable help and encouragement, without which this history might well have remained unpublished.

Especial thanks are due to Mr. George Cooke, who wrote the booklet "Snowshill in Gloucestershire" for the National Trust in 1979. He generously made all his material available to me and read the draft, making various helpful comments. Mr. Michael Jessup, the Reverend Robert Hannay, Colonel Geoffrey Powell and Mr. and Mrs. William B. Wilkerson of Texas, U.S.A. were also kind enough to read the draft. I am most grateful to them all for their various suggestions and comments but must add that they are in no way responsible for the mistakes which undoubtedly remain.

Others who have helped me in a variety of ways include the Reverend Michael Bland M.A., who kindly translated sections of the "Landboc" from the Latin, my daughter, Claire, who drew the map of ancient roads and tracks, Mr. George Diston of Tewkesbury and formerly of Snowshill, Mr. Claude Arkell and Mr. Valentine Teale of Donnington Brewery, Dr. S. P. Needham of the British Museum, Dr. Christopher Dyer of Birmingham University, the staff of the "Evesham Journal", the staff of both Cheltenham and Gloucester Public Libraries, the staff of the Worcestershire Record Office and most particularly the staff of the Gloucestershire Record Office.

I am grateful to Buchan & Enright, Publishers, Limited for permission to quote from "John Buchan — A Memoir" by William Buchan, 1982. A passage from "The Gloucestershire Landscape" by H. P. R. Finberg, (from "The Making of the English Landscape" edited by W. G. Hoskins) © 1975 by H. P. R. Finberg is reprinted by permission of Hodder & Stoughton Limited. The extract from Domesday is reproduced by kind permission from the Phillimore edition of

Domesday Book (General Editor John Morris), volume 15 Gloucestershire (County Editor John Moore), published by Phillimore & Company Limited, Shopwyke Hall, Chichester, West Sussex.

If there are any instances in which I have failed to establish whether an item is in copyright, I can only apologise.

Finally I thank my husband, Christopher, who has helped me at every stage of the research, writing, correcting and typing of this village history, and my daughter, Frances, who has been so patient with us both.

List of Maps and Illustrations

List of Plates

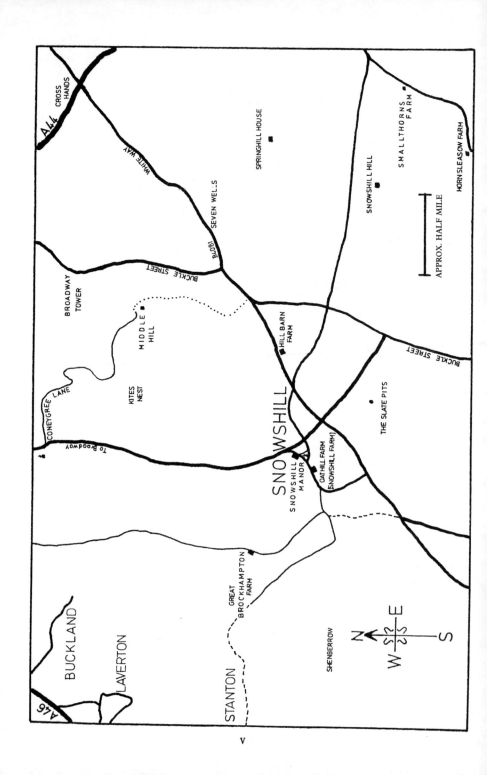

Prehistory to Domesday

Well over three thousand years ago, before the time of Moses, men were living and tending their sheep in the area of Snowshill in Gloucestershire, a small Cotswold village nestling in the wolds beneath the brow of Oat Hill, two and a half miles to the South of the Worcestershire village of Broadway. Although Snowshill is a small community of under two hundred inhabitants, there are two good reasons for its long history. The first is that the area is blessed with an ample supply of spring water and the second is its close proximity to the probable course of two prehistoric trackways.

Bronze Age Barrows

In January 1881 Snowshill was placed firmly on the archaeological map of Britain with the excavation by the Rev. William Greenwell M.A., D.C.L., F.R.S., of a Bronze Age barrow, situated about half a mile to the South-West of the village in a field then farmed by George Hyatt.[1] Six barrows, and a possible seventh are recorded within the parish. Two of these barrows were believed to have been opened long ago and another was thought to have contained bronze spear heads and other articles. The remaining barrow opened by Greenwell was found to be of such interest that its contents are now in the British Museum, much to the regret of such local historians as E. A. B. Barnard, at one time President of the Worcestershire Archaeological Society, who wished that they could have been on permanent exhibit in Cheltenham. The contents consisted of two superbly made bronze daggers, a crutch-headed bronze pin and a perforated axe-hammer of stone, together with a skeleton of a man, believed to be a warrior. Dr. S. P. Needham of the British Museum dates the artefacts between 1600 and 1400 B.C. A fuller description of Greenwell's barrow and its contents is contained in Appendix I.

Bronze Dagger

Bronze Dagger

Stone Axe-hammer

Bronze Pin

Artefacts found in the barrow at Snowshill

Trackways

Snowshill was an obvious site for early settlement as it not only provided an abundance of spring water but it also lay close to the crossing point of two probable ancient trackways. All but a few prehistoric trackways are impossible to date, or even to trace with any degree of certainty, but the surmised trackway which runs closest to Snowshill is the White Way, part of the so-called Jurassic Way, said to have linked the Humber with the Bristol Channel or Portland. Although the archaeologist Christopher Taylor questions its existance as a prehistoric Jurassic Way,[2] the White Way was undoubtedly in existence in mediaeval times and many archaeologists believe that it was a prehistoric road and a highway in all senses and that it came up from the South-West to Andoversford from whence the main Stone Age route carried on via Stow-on-the-Wold to the Rollright Stones and on up to the North-East. G. R. Crosher, in his study of Cotswold ways, believes that the Neolithic people more probably took a drier route to the Rollright Stones curving North of where Moreton-in-Marsh now stands.[3] This route from Andoversford via Stumps Cross runs in a relatively straight line past Snowshill some five hundred yards from the Bronze Age burial ground and, even though it may be impossible to date the track with any degree of certainty, there is little doubt that it formed part of one of the Dark Age salt ways. With a spur straight on to Campden, it was destined to become, in the seventeenth century, one of Gloucestershire's four most important roads.

About three quarters of a mile to the East of Snowshill, the postulated Jurassic Way is crossed by another probable ancient trackway which according to the eminent local archaeologist, Mrs. Helen O'Neil, probably ran from Bourton-on-the-Water to the Welsh Marches.[4] Known since the seventeenth century as Buckle Street, a corruption of Buggildway or Bugghilde Streete, it is thought to have been named after an Anglo-Saxon lady, Burghild, in the early eighth century. The Saxon origins of its name have sometimes given rise to Buckle Street being regarded as a Saxon road but this is improbable as there are no fewer than ten known Bronze Age barrows along its path between Snowshill and Bourton-on-the-Water. There is, therefore, every likelihood that Snowshill lay at the crossing point of two important Bronze Age lines of communication.

Ryknild Street is a third probable prehistoric trackway which is known to have been straightened and surfaced by the Romans and indeed appears on the Ordnance Survey map of Roman Roads. Like Buckle Street it links Bourton-on-the-Water and the Fosse Way with Bidford-on-Avon, but by a more direct route. It crosses the probable Jurassic Way about two miles East of Snowshill and linked the Roman settlements of Bourton-on-the-Water, Lower Slaughter and Dorn.[5]

3

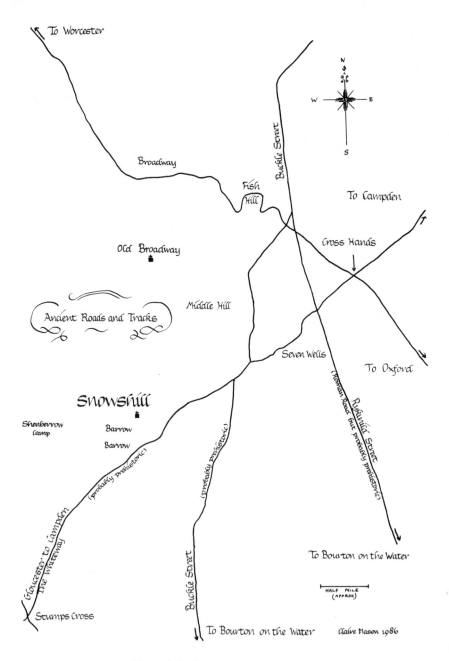

Map of Ancient Roads and Tracks

Iron Age and Romano-British Settlement

Shenberrow Hill Camp, midway between Snowshill and neighbouring Stanton, is the next evidence of human settlement in the area. Although primarily an Iron Age and later a Romano-British settlement, the finding of Beaker pottery suggests that the site was also known to early Bronze Age people which is hardly surprising as it is less than a mile from the known Bronze Age site at Snowshill. Shenberrow was probably initially settled by people of the Iron Age in c300 B.C. and is thought to have continued to be occupied into the first century B.C. with later Romano-British occupation in the second century A.D. The camp may have begun as an open settlement but, as times grew more violent, the first defensive rampart would have been built, followed later by a second outer rampart. Standing on the Jurassic ridge, Shenberrow is one of a series of Iron Age forts along the whole length of the Cotswold escarpment.[6] The site was partially excavated in July 1935 by students from the Universities of Cambridge and London and the results of their excavation are described in Appendix II.

With archaeological evidence for Bronze Age, Iron Age and Romano-British settlement of the Snowshill area, there is a strong possibility that there has been continuous human habitation of Snowshill from the Bronze Age to the present day. W. G. Hoskins, who may be described as the pioneer of landscape-history, wrote in his introduction to H. P. R. Finberg's book "The Gloucestershire Landscape",

> I think it is highly likely that in some favoured parts of England farming has gone on in an unbroken continuity since the Iron Age, perhaps even since the Bronze Age; and that many of our villages were first settled at the same time. In other words, that underneath our old villages, and underneath the older parts of these villages, there may well be evidence of habitation going back for some two or three thousand years. Conquests only meant in most places a change of landlord for better or for worse, but farming went on unbroken, for even conquerors would have starved without its continuous activity. We have so far failed to find this continuity of habitation because sites have been built over and over again and have never been wholly cleared and examined by trained archaeologists.[7]

There is every reason to believe that all this applied in the case of Snowshill.

Saint Patrick and Gildas, the two Roman Britons whose writings are our chief source of information on fifth century Britain, take it for granted that all their fellow countrymen were Christian.[8] It is likely that there was a bishop in Corinium by the end of the fourth century but whether Christianity had reached such upland villages as Snowshill at this stage is uncertain.

The Roman garrisons were withdrawn in 410 and by 446 links with Rome were severed. The departure of the Romans marked an end of coinage and an organised pottery industry so there is little for the archaeologist to find from this period and such as can be found is difficult to date. However it is likely that rural settlement continued as before and did not change greatly when the pagan Saxons invaded Britain in the sixth century. By 525 the Saxons had settled in Fairford and probably, in the main, took over existing settlements and followed existing lines of communication. Cotswold names are primarily Saxon and Snowshill is no exception. In Domesday it appears as Snawesille. Opinions differ as to whether Snaw was the name of a long forgotten Angle or Saxon, or whether the name meant then, as now, "hill of snow". In any event, the propensity of snow to linger in the folds of the hill no doubt contributed to the evolution of the name to Snowshill.

The Dark Ages

In 628 the Saxons were forced to come to terms with Penda,[9] the last pagan King of Mercia who allotted Gloucestershire, the Oxfordshire Cotswolds, Worcestershire and some of Warwickshire to two Northumbrian Christian princes who had assisted him. For five generations this dynasty ruled what came to be known as the Kingdom of Hwicce. It was a kingdom within and subject to the powerful Kingdom of Mercia and this state of affairs prevailed until Hwicce and the rest of Mercia submitted to King Alfred c877-883.

The surviving British population in the Kingdom of Hwicce shared with their new rulers a common faith in Christianity, and, in country districts such as Snowshill, Christians met for worship in the open air in circular burial grounds enclosed by an earthen rampart or dry stone wall. After a while a simple structure would be raised to protect the priest and in time a small church would be built.[10]

Theodore of Tarsus was consecrated Archbishop of Canterbury in 668[11] and it was he who began to divide England into parishes at the end of the seventh century. It was also under Theodore that the Diocese of Worcester was founded in 669 though not established till 780. The boundaries of the diocese roughly coincided with those of the Kingdom of Hwicce and the early bishops bore the title "Episcopus Hwiccorum". The Venerable Bede records that two rulers of the Hwicce, Eanhere and Eanfrid, had become Christian in c675.

The Benedictine Abbey of St. Mary at Winchcombe was founded by King Kenulf of Mercia in c798[12] and it housed the archives of the Mercian royal house. Winchcombe had become a seat of the Mercian

6

royalty and capital of the county of Wincelcumshire which was later to become incorporated into Gloucestershire, in the reign of King Canute c1007-1017.

King Kenulf gave the manor, tithes and the chaplaincy of Snowshill, together with the manor, tithes and advowson of Stanton to the Abbey at Winchcombe in either 811 or 821. Opinions differ as to which of these two dates is correct. The Abbey was one of the richest in the country and Snowshill provided it with seven hides of land, equivalent to eight hundred and forty acres, which then, as at all times, was used mainly for sheep grazing.

In the early ninth century, Mercian power waned and the kingdom came under the overlordship of Wessex. Alfred came to the throne of Wessex in 871 when English fortunes were low due to a barrage of Viking incursions and he managed to achieve a balance of power. It is unlikely that the turbulance of the Dark Ages had very much impact on a small rural community such as the Manor of Snowshill and we may be sure that they were far more concerned with the incidence of disease and the unpredictability of the weather, with its effect on their crops, than with the various shifts of power and influence.

Snowshill under the
Abbey of Winchcombe

Domesday

After the Conquest, William claimed the whole land of England as forfeited to him and laid down the principle, which remains part of English law to this day, that the Crown alone is the owner of land and that all others are but tenants holding their land directly or indirectly from the Crown. William retained much of England in his own hands. There were royal manors in nearly every shire and the King was by far the greatest landlord. The rest he granted to his chief followers, lay and ecclesiastical, who became tenants-in-chief, owing service to the Crown. One of the richest and most powerful of these was the Abbey of Winchcombe which had held Snowshill since early in the ninth century. In present day terms the Abbot of Winchcombe would have been a multi-millionaire and his annual income of £1000 would be worth about £1,000,000 today.

In 1085 William ordered that a survey should be made of the whole country to find out what and how much each landholder held in land and livestock and what it was worth both then and in 1066. He wanted to know how many villagers, smallholders and slaves there were and how many plough-teams they had, together with information about woodland, meadows, pasture, mills and fishponds. The enormous task of compiling Domesday was completed in less than a year and it has provided us with an unparalleled source of information about medieval England.

Shires had long been divided into hundreds which in turn were divided into manors. These were areas of land and political units, comprising a ruler and dependent population. Domesday therefore is a record of manors and not of villages, although these frequently, as in the case of Snowshill, gradually evolved on the same site.

The Domesday entry for Snowshill reads, in translation:

LAND OF THE CHURCH OF WINCHCOMBE in HOLFORD Hundred SNOWSHILL, 7 hides which pay tax. In Lordship 3 ploughs; 12 villagers and two smallholders with 6 ploughs. 6 slaves. The value is and was 100s.[1]

From this we learn that the manor consisted of some 840 acres, almost all of which is likely to have been under cultivation. The woodland will have been cleared long before in common with most of the surrounding area. The Cotswolds and in particular Snowshill have always been rightly associated with sheep but the importance of arable farming must not be underestimated. A two field system was operated whereby at any one time half the land was under cultivation while the other half was being grazed by sheep, who in turn enriched the land for further cultivation. The two main crops were barley, used for a multiplicity of purposes, including bread and beer, and dredge which was a mixture of barley and oats.

Although in most hundreds, a villager would normally farm a virgate (30 acres), in Holford hundred the average was two virgates, while the smallholders had just a few acres.

Domesday was not a census but it does nevertheless enable us to make reasonably accurate estimates of population on the basis that, apart from slaves who were normally unmarried, each household consisted of an average of five persons, that is to say a nuclear family of four and one other relative. Priests were not listed separately but came into the category of villagers, usually being married with children. The priesthood only became celibate in the thirteenth century.

We may assume that the population of Snowshill in 1086 was about eighty. Although the population of Campden was about three hundred, the average population of a manor at Domesday was between fifty-three and two hundred, so it is clear that Snowshill was by no means an insignificant place. Its value between 1066 and 1086 was stable at one hundred shillings, again a not insignificant sum compared with other manors. This value was an estimate of what the landlord, which in the case of Snowshill was the Abbey of Winchcombe, would receive in money and kind from his tenants.

The three main categories of countrymen, villagers, smallholders and slaves, were each represented at Snowshill. Gloucestershire had the highest proportion of slaves in the land and there were six of these unfortunates in Snowshill. Slaves had no legal rights and held no land, earning their keep as hired labour, probably mainly on the demesne lands. Around 1100, slavery gave way to serfdom. Serfs were still in legal subjection to the landlord but they could hold land. There were two smallholders in the manor but the largest category were the villagers of whom there were twelve. This means that Snowshill was divided into eleven or twelve farms each of approximately sixty acres, together with two smallholdings and the demesne lands of rather less than a hundred acres.

Manor and Parish

Life in mediaeval Snowshill must have been arduous and comfortless with the routine of hard labour interrupted only by the occasional visit to market and by church festivals. Nevertheless this was not subsistance farming and villagers owed services and half of what they produced to the landlord, the Abbot of Winchcombe and a tenth to the church in tithes. The church came to regard the basic unit of agriculture as the chief product of the area from which the tithes were drawn, which in the case of Snowshill was wool. Snowshill Manor was assessed as 1000 sheep in the summer at 1d and 500 sheep in the winter at 4d.

Tithes were "the tenth part of the increase yearly arising from the profits of lands, stocks upon lands and the industry of parishioners, payable for the maintenance of the parish priest, by everyone who has things titheable, if he cannot show special exemption." Tithes were usually divided into three classes, predial, mixed and personal. Predial tithes were such as arose immediately from the ground, such as lambs, wool, eggs etc. Personal tithes were on the fruit of labour and industry. Tithes were first legally recognised in 786 but were an unsatisfactory tax which did little to enhance the prestige of the clergy. Towards the end of the seventeenth century tithes were by statute commuted for regular payments of money and in the eighteenth century, at the time of the Inclosure Acts, tithes were frequently commuted, as at Snowshill, in return for allotments of land. Tithes as well as scutage (the obligation to pay money in lieu of providing military service) and rents were paid at Snowshill Manor Court.

Snowshill has never had a rector or vicar of its own, but it has sometimes had a curate. It has always been part of the rectory of Stanton cum Snowshill. Although the rectors can only be traced back to 1269, there are records as early as 1183 of tithes being used for restoring Winchcombe Abbey and its cloisters which had suffered a disastrous fire in 1151. The inhabitants of Snowshill were required to pay tithes for this purpose until at least 1206, under pain of excommunication.

The Abbots of Winchcombe kept detailed records of their lands and estates and fortunately many of these have survived and are known as the Sherborne Muniments. In 1903, D. Royce edited and published many of these records in the "Landboc, sive Registrum Monasterii de Winchelcumba", thus making accessible a valuable source of material. It is inevitable however that the "Landboc" only provides disconnected glimpses of mediaeval Snowshill. One point that the "Landboc" illustrates clearly is that bureaucratic verbosity is nothing new as shown in the following examples:

Confirmation of Bishop Baldwin about these tithes

To all the faithful to whom these presents shall come, We Baldwin by divine permission minister of the church of Worcester, greetings in the Lord. Be it noted that we have made by our appointed officials, an inquisition about the tithes of Stanton and Snowshill: and it is found from this inquisition that the two tithe sheaves of the aforesaid villages pertain to the use of monks of Winchcombe: that lest in time doubts may arise again, this present signature and our seal, confirm the same.

To this witness William Archdeacon of Gloucester
    Master Samson
    Master Silurno
    Peter of Withington
    Master Godfrey
    John of Exeter
    William Prudhomme

And in process of time, after the retirement, so it is said, of Richard Archbishop of Canterbury /1174-1185/ the successor of the blessed Saint Thomas /a Becket/ the aforesaid Baldwin, Bishop of Worcester was translated to the Metropolitan See of the same church of Canterbury, confirmed the aforesaid tithes by Archiepiscopal authority in the same way.

Confirmation of Baldwin Archbishop of Canterbury about these tithes

To all the faithful to whom these present writings shall come, Baldwin, by the grace of God, Archbishop of Canterbury, Primate of All England, greeting in the Lord. To everyone to whom our notices shall come, with regard to the church of Worcester, of which we had formerly the administration, about the tithes of Stanton and of Snowshill, and to whom they pertain, we have instructed diligent inquisition to be made, from which, with our authority, we have confirmed that the aforesaid tithes of two sheaves pertains to our beloved sons the monks of Winchcombe. And that therefore, as by our authority then committed to us, with good reason, is now by our present authority, confirmed.

And as a precaution they are not injured, for the greater security, against malignant machinations they may have unassailable title by the confirmation of the Apostolic See.

Confirmation of Pope Urban about these tithes
and of the pension of Enstone and of Winchcombe

Urban /1185-1187/ bishop, servant of the servants of God, to
our beloved sons the Abbot and Monks of Winchcombe,
greeting and Apostolic blessing. What seems reasonable to
us, and our soul inclines to concede, we bring into effect.
Accordingly, in the Lord, beloved brethren, by our just
decision, the tithes of Stanton and Snowshill, which are in
the presentation of our venerable brother Baldwin now
Archbishop of Canterbury, formerly of Worcester, are
defined . . . . . .
Dated Verona 13th Kalends of January.[2]

In 1251, the Abbot purchased from the Crown a charter of Free
Warren for Snowshill and all his other manors. This was the right to
keep and hunt animals within an enclosure or warren. A fine of £10 was
imposed for trespass or entrance in pursuit of game, which must have
been a formidable deterrent.

The Episcopal Register for the Diocese of Worcester records the
institution of Robert of Northleach as clerk to the Church of Stanton on
the 15th August 1269 but makes no mention of Snowshill, in common
with another entry for 1278. However in 1290, Snowshill is firmly on
the diocesan map with a record of the induction of "Henry de Dydebrok,
priest to the Church of Staunton with the Chapel of Snaweshull at the
presentation of the Abbot of Wynch. 4th Dec."

Bishop Reynold's Register of 1308-1313 makes several references to
Snowshill. In 1309 Richard de Snaweshull received a Letter Dismissary
and in 1310 Gilbert de Snaweshull was ordained. Gilbert is further
listed as a deacon in 1312 and in the following year he was ordained
priest in Worcester Cathedral.

An interesting incident occurred in 1312 when Snowshill was the
venue chosen to resolve a dispute between the Abbot and Convent of
Winchcombe and Master Elyas de Gayton, rector of the Church of
Hazleton and the Chapel of Yaneworth and their predecessors. It
concerned land, tithes, common pasture in woods, meadows and other
several pastures and commons and things touching on the status of the
said Church. The parties had appeared before the Official and, through
the intervention of common friends, agreed to submit the matter to the
Bishop. This "submission" was sealed by the parties and the Official "at
Snowshull, iii Non Oct. 1312". This incident would suggest that there
was a manor house of adequate size and importance to provide a setting
for this encounter.[3]

At this period there are two records in the "Landboc" concerning a
certain Master Richard of Snowshill who was a Notary Public and clerk

to Winchcombe Abbey. In July 1310 he was awarded an annual clerk's robe and food when he was in Winchcombe for "transmarine and cismarine" services. As a clerk, he had an important liturgical function and had been sent on missions at home and abroad. The "robe" may have been a tunicle to wear at Mass. In August 1324 for further transmarine and cismarine services and mindful of a sum of money and other benefits received, Abbot Richard rewarded Richard of Snowshill most lavishly. He received the chamber East of the Abbey gate with its garderobe, with leave to have for life a new chamber built at his own cost of "our" timber. He also had a stable for two horses which was large enough to hold three cartloads of hay delivered by the Abbey. He was to receive generous supplies of provisions including bread, beer, meat, fish, mustard, sauces and garlic. If however he was absent for a year then he would receive twenty shillings in lieu. In addition to a number of other things, he was also to receive a specially high quality overcoat, fur lined and with a fur hood. The extent of these rewards would suggest that he had his own interests and those of the Abbot rather more to heart than those of the tenants of Snowshill.[4]

In 1319, when Cotswold wool production was still at its height, the Abbot assigned the income of Snowshill Manor to the Priory of St. Ebrulf at Uttica in Normandy. Both Sir Robert Atkyns in his "Ancient and Present State of Gloucestershire" (1712) and Samuel Rudder in his "A New History of Gloucestershire" (1799) refer to this assignment but the reasons for it are far from clear. The Abbey nevertheless continued to manage the affairs of the tenants. Each May the Abbot moved his household to Sherborne, five miles West of Burford, for a month, bringing his flocks from Snowshill, Charlton Abbots, Hawling and Roel to be washed in Sherborne Brook before shearing. These flocks had been greatly enlarged during the thirteenth century to meet the export demand from the Netherlands and Italy.

The following extract from the "Landboc" concerns a certain Nicholas.

> Be it known to whom these presents may come, that I, Henry, by the grace of God, Abbot of Winchcombe and the convent, concede to Nicholas and his heirs, one hide in Snowshill with a combe, to be held of us freely and quietly from all service, except the service of our Lord the King, and that the said Nicholas and his heirs, make the aforesaid, like the others in the village, as one of his hides. For this concession the aforesaid Nicholas and his heirs shall render to our church, for every year, on the feast of Saint Kenelm, thirteen shillings. And furthermore, we concede that he shall have

eight of his own oxen to plough his allotment in the pasture of our lordship, except in our meadows. To this witness

Wiliam de Tracy
Alexander the Butler
Robert Russel
Alan, clergyman of Slaughter
Robert of Hazelton
Robert of Dicklesdona
and H. his heir
William of Sherborne
Robert of Slaughter
G. of Shipton
Nicholas of Bruern
Robert of Dowdeswell

and all the court of the lord Abbot who were there that day.[5]

John le Freman is a name which recurs in the records of fourteenth century Snowshill. Around the turn of the century he had to pay scutage on a hide in aid of Edwards's wars in Wales and Scotland. The name appears again in 1327 at the head of the Lay Sudsidy Roll, by which time one suspects that he held rather less than a hide. The Lay Subsidy Roll lists villagers and their tax assessments but the practice of listing villagers individually ceased after 1334.

John le Freman	12d	William atte Yate	14d
William Morcok	14d	Adam le Quarrier	18d
William Broun	20d	Sarra de Brockhampton	12d
Raduo Michel	20d		

It will be recalled that at Domesday there were twelve villagers and here, in 1327, only seven are listed as tax payers. Nevertheless there were some twenty-five or so tenants at the time so it must be assumed that the rest were extremely poor. It is also interesting to note that there was now a quarrier in the village and he appears to have been comparatively prosperous. However, around about this time things began to go badly for farmers. It is thought that bad weather was producing bad harvests and indeed 1341 is recorded as having been an exceptionally bad year for Snowshill. John le Freman's one hundred and twenty acres had apparently dwindled to a mere fifteen and he was unable to pay his tax. No mercy was shown and he was obliged to hand over his brass pot in lieu. There is evidence that the depression in the wool industry at this time with its resulting poverty had led to increased lawlessness around Campden. Percy C. Rushen in "The History and Antiquities of Campden", which was published in 1899, refers to the appointment of a commission of oyer and terminer on 21st November, 1327, to enquire into a complaint that William de Snoushull and others had carried away the goods of Nicholas de Lavyngton and Nicholas de Turril at Caumpeden.

The Black Death

In 1349 things went from bad to worse. Disaster struck Snowshill when the Black Death killed approximately half the population and only fourteen tenants survived. Of these a further four died in a second outbreak of the plague in 1361. Curiously all these victims were survived and succeeded by their widows. With its population halved and its menfolk so severely depleted, it is likely that a number of Snowshill's cottages fell into disrepair and decay. The plague also took a terrible toll on Winchcombe Abbey which found itself unable to support its community. In 1358 the Abbot's Roll states that "it is burdened with great debt and is so miserably improverished that it is necessary to place its temporalities into the hands of a commission of the Crown."

Two years later, on January 23rd 1360, an entry reads, "it would be no harm to the King or any other to allow the said William (de Fravilesworth) and Eleanor to grant one messuage (12d rent and four virgates of land four acres excepted) in Snoweshille and Little Wormington which Julienne Freeman holds for term of her life to find a monk to celebrate for the health and the souls, when they are departed this life, of the said William and Eleanor every day in the said Abbey for ever. The premises are held by the said Abbey and of the said William de Fravilesworth and Eleanor his wife by a rent of 13s 4d. in silver and suit every year at the Abbey Court of Snowshille and are worth 6s. in silver beyond the above rent".[6] Clearly the Abbot was glad to accept extra land in return for a daily mass.

The rights of the Priory of St. Ebrulf in Normandy were terminated in 1415 when alien monasteries were divested of their lands in England and Snowshill Manor returned once more to the Abbey of Winchcombe.

The early fifteenth century saw a transfer from cultivation to pasture, due to shortage of manpower as a consequence of the plague. As there were fewer men, holdings tended to grow larger and the authority of the landlord waned. Yeoman farmers prospered and they acquired more possessions. Their flocks averaged around three hundred sheep each and indeed there are reports that at one time there were too many sheep at Snowshill.

1539 saw the Dissolution of Winchcombe Abbey and, as a consequence, Snowshill Manor became the property of the Crown. A further consequence of the Reformation was that Snowshill and other parishes in the Deanery of Campden moved out of the Diocese of Worcester and into the new Diocese of Gloucester.

Snowshill from Tudor times until 1800

The Tudor Manor

In the fifteenth century the Dastons (or Distons) are first recorded in Snowshill and there have been descendants in the village until the death of Leslie Diston in 1985. They were an ancient family who owned Dumbleton and leased land in Broadway. Indeed Ann Daston (born 1528) of Broadway Court became the largest landowner in Broadway with 2900 acres out of 4900. In 1467, John Daston was Lord of the Manor of Snowshill and in 1591 Richard Daston presented the new rector, Robert Clutterbrucke, on his institution. It would seem likely that other Dastons were Lords of the Manor during the intervening period.

There is a likelihood that a Saxon house was built in the ninth century and that it was rebuilt in the reign of Henry VI around 1450 but it was early in the sixteenth century that the Northern part of the present Manor House was built. It is perhaps not surprising that a substantial house should have been built at Snowshill at this period as times were good for sheep farming and flocks were expanding, due to a rise in the price of wool between 1510 and 1520. In the sixteenth century there are a number of references to the Sambage or Sambach family, who were clearly well established in the village, as were the Stanleys. Two centuries later, two generations of the Sambaches owned Snowshill Manor and the Stanleys remained in the village until the first part of the twentieth century. In January 1558, the Will of "John Sambage of Snoweshyll" was "approved". There is a further interesting record in the Hockaday Abstracts:-

> 1563 Thomas Sambage and Thomas Newman church-wardens of Snosell present as follows
>> That the church and windowes be amiss
>> Also Goodwithe Phelps wydowe doth not make
>> the churche wall which belongeth unto her.
>> Otherwise well.

Thomas Sambage's Will was proved in 1604.

Henry VIII consigned the Manor to Catherine Parr in 1543 as part of her dower. Two months after Henry VIII's death in 1547, Catherine Parr married Thomas Seymour, Lord Sudeley, to whom she had previously been betrothed, and they came to live at the recently restored castle at Sudeley. The marriage was short-lived as Catherine died in childbirth at Sudeley in 1548. Snowshill was but one of nineteen manors acquired by Lord Sudeley, and in any event he had little opportunity to enjoy his property because he was executed in 1549 as a result of trying to supplant his brother, the Duke of Somerset and Protector. Snowshill Manor reverted to the Crown and Edward VI granted it to the unscrupulous John Dudley, Earl of Warwick, who was created Duke of Northumberland in 1551. He too had little opportunity for enjoyment as two years later he was sent to the Tower and finally executed for supporting Lady Jane Grey. Yet again, but for the last time, the Manor reverted to the Crown and on this occasion Mary Tudor gave it to Francis Bulstrode. At approximately the same time, Queen Mary gave the Manor of Stanton together with the patronage of the Church at Stanton and the Chapel at Snowshill to John Eliot. He obtained a licence to alienate them to Thomas Dolman and later his son, John Dolman, had livery of the advowson of the Church in 1553.

The Tudor Church and Village

In 1561, Francis and his wife Ann Bulstrode "sold the Manor with the advowsons and appurtenances in Brockhampton and Wormington to Henry Willoughby," to whom, in the same year, Queen Elizabeth granted the livery of the Manor. Willoughby was probably the first owner of the Manor to live in the village and truly fulfil the role of the Lord of the Manor. It is recorded that on "October 10, 1570, Henry Willoughbie of Worcester diocese, gent, prayed that no one be admitted or instituted to the parish church of Snoweshill without his being called in his right of patronage." Two years later, further Church dilapidations were reported:-

1572 Snoweshill Presentment
July — The chauncell lacketh mossinge soe that the rayne and snowe enter in the default of the person of Staunton. There is defect in the churche yard gate in the saied persons default — October 23.
The person doth minister service at Snoweshill and Staunton in one daye.[1]

We do not know what effect, if any, the frequent change of ownership of the Manor had on the people of Snowshill although it certainly does seem to have been a period of growth in population as the number of communicants rose from 130 in 1551 to 176 in 1603. This was in line with the national trend for that period. The sixteenth century started well for sheep farmers with a rise in the price of wool which encouraged an expansion in flocks and pasturage between 1510 and 1520. This was followed by a depression and then a further boom

17

which lasted until 1551 when there was another serious depression. A general decline then occurred in the rearing of sheep in the Cotswolds and there was a switch from wool to meat and cheese production, although we cannot be sure that this trend was necessarily followed in Snowshill. It was also a period of rampant inflation and the purchasing power of wages reached its lowest point in 1597.

It appears that Henry Willoughby sold the Manor to Miles Stander, John Popham, George Fettiplace and Matthew Smith of the Middle Temple, London, in 1565 but this date seems questionable since, as has already been noted, Willoughby was still exercising his right of patronage in 1570.

The Warne (or Warren) family came from Newton, Suffolk, and settled around Snowshill and Stanton at the time of the Dissolution in 1539. It is thought possible that John and Thomas Warne even then leased the house and lands from the various owners of Snowshill, although the earliest recorded lease is dated 1565. By 1575, however, the Warnes had bought Snowshill Manor. By then they must have been old men because, in 1577, Thomas's grandson, also called Thomas, bought land in Stanton from Thomas Dolman and built Warren House. Snowshill Manor remained in the Warne family until 1638, although there is a record of another John Warne, buried at Snowshill, who died in 1728. During the Warne ownership, some structural changes were made to the Manor House. The Great Hall had previously been a lofty room extending to the roof but, in around 1600, a first floor bedroom was constructed above the hall. At this period it was a long narrow house, one room deep, facing across the valley to the West. A tithe barn was attached to the Northern end but we do know the date of its construction. Most of the mullion windows and drip mouldings date from this period, although the windows with cross infil on the South Front elevation are late seventeenth century or later.

It was also during the Warne's ownership of the Manor that a sinister episode occurred which gave rise to one of Snowshill's ghost stories. As a result of what was described in a subsequent Bill of Complaint in the Court of Star Chamber as "an ungodly plott", Anthony Palmer, a handsome twenty year old servant, and others are alleged to have assembled at Elmley Castle on St. Valentine's Eve, 1604, armed with swords, daggers and pistols and, at eleven o'clock at night, forceably carried away the fifteen year old orphan heiress Ann Parsons from the home of William Savage where she was then living "under the tuition and government" of Richard Daston, and took her to Snowshill. Ann's fortune had arisen from the will of her mother Goodith Parsons who had appointed Richard Daston her tutor and both him and William Savage as executors. The latter had clearly seen the advantage of a marriage of Ann into his own family and she had become betrothed to his son, George, but it is unlikely that Ann had needed much persuasion to accompany Palmer with whom she was probably infatuated. At midnight, a clandestine marriage is alleged to have taken place at Snowshill Manor in the room above the Great Hall, now known as Ann's Room, with the obvious co-operation of John Warne. The ceremony was performed by the Reverend Richard Stone, Vicar of St. Eadburgha's, Broadway, "contrary to the laws of God and the Church". No record of this marriage exists and the detail of the story is based on the Bill of Complaint for abduction and unlawful marriage presented to the Star Chamber. There is no record of the outcome of the proceedings and history does not relate whether the romance of Ann and Anthony had a happy ending. The local belief, however, that Ann's Room is haunted by her ghost does not suggest happiness.

There is record of further clandestine activity in Snowshill during the Warne era. In 1612, Thomas Preston, a labourer and Humphrey Eaton, also a labourer, both late of Blockley, were indicted at Worcestershire Quarter Sessions for the theft of two white swans belonging to John Warne.

The Parish Register

The Snowshill section of the parish register is entitled "Snowshull Capella Tempore Roberti Cluttesbrook Rector Ibid Anno Dni 1572". In 1591 a similar title records the coming of Lawrence Banks to the living. Unfortunately this section only goes up to 1604 so the entries are very incomplete. There appears to have been a curate living in the village in 1572 and there is known to have been one in 1623. The records indicate that there was very little association between the neighbouring villages of Stanton and Snowshill as the surnames of the inhabitants are quite distinct with the exception of the Warren (or Warne) family who originated in Snowshill. This separateness continues to this day. During the period from 1572 to 1603, there were 83 Baptisms, 27 Marriages and 43 Burials in Snowshill.

"Men and Armour for Gloucestershire in 1608"

"Men and Armour for Gloucestershire in 1608" gives us some insight into the lives and occupations of the inhabitants of the village. Under "Snowshill" it lists:-

> John Warne sonne of Thomas Warne, gent. 1.p.
> John Lawrance 2.p.)
> John Brumpstone 1.p.) servants to the said
> Allen Winslee 1.ca.) Thomas Warne gent.
> Rowland Smith 2.ca.)
> Henry Tasker 2.ca.)
> Robert Mayor servant to Thomas Numne 1.ca.
> Thomas Sambage husbandman, 2.ca.sub.
> Nycholas Izod his servant. 1.ca.
> Thomas Woodward husbandman. 2.py.
> Thomas Haddocke husbandman. 2.ca.tr.
> Davyd Evans taylor. 1.ca.
> John Joyne apprentice to Davyd Evans. 1.ca.
> Richard Wells wever. 2.ca.
> Richard Bussell. 3.py.
> Richard Carpenter shepeerd.
> William Buttel shepeerd. 1.p.
> William Clarke shepeerd. 1.m.
> William Ward
>   servant to the said William Clarke. 1.m.
> William Goddard mason. tr.
> Thomas Bromley his apprentice. 1.m.
> Robert Goddard mason. 1.ca.
> Thomas Cowmedowe. 1.ca.

Inhabytants chardged with the finding of Armour not before mentioned
> Thomas Warne gent. unable in body hath two Calyvers furnished sub.

Also the said Tythinge standeth chardged with the finding of one Calyver with the fur.[2]

The abbreviations in this list indicate the ages of the men concerned and the weapons they were capable of carrying and are explained in Appendix III.

Thomas Warne clearly kept enough staff at the Manor House to live comfortably and then, as throughout, sheep farming was the main industry. Again the unusual name Sambage appears, almost certainly another forebear of William Sambach who in 1712 bought the Manor from Will Wall (or Walle), grandson of the Will Wall of London who, in 1638, had bought it for five thousand and fifty pounds. The indenture of

June 7th, 1638, described Snowshill Manor as "the Manor House Farm or Grainage of Snowshill" and gives a detailed list of the fields which then comprised the estate. The list is set out in Appendix IV.

The Tithe Book 1624-1744

Another source of information about this period is the tithe book. Not many tithe books still exist but fortunately Stanton's book for the period 1624 to 1744 has survived.

The sheep pastures in Snowshill are detailed as follows:-
John Ardway of Broadway, one hundred sheeps pastures on the Hill.

Thomas Blissard of Laberton	70 sheep
Widdow Alice Blissard	60 sheep
Young Richard Fisher of the Cross	30 sheep
Edmund Ray	20 sheep
James Hale	20 sheep
John Tisoe of Buckland	40 sheep
John Brown of Broadway	40 sheep
Thomas Bridge of Laberton	20 sheep
	400 sheep[3]

The rector, who was inevitably something of a farmer as well as a parson, also recorded that on Holy Cross Day, the 3rd May, 1632, "my brother paid me fifteen shillings for the winter tithes of Stanton and twelve shillings for the half tithes of his close, but betwixt Holy Rood Day and Michaelmas following he paid me neither tithe-wool nor any recompense for it, neither for Snowshill nor Stanton."

The seventeenth century started with a period of high inflation which only began to slow down in the 1620s. 1614 saw the then highest recorded export of cloth but eight years later this was halved. 1629-35 were good years but these in turn were followed by bad harvests and considerable distress. This was also the period when the two earliest surviving rows of cottages in Snowshill, those opposite the Manor and Rose Cottage and The Old Shop, were built. Before about 1570, stone, though so abundant, had been a building material reserved for churches and larger houses, while farmhouses, cottages and barns were timber framed, timber likewise being plentiful. It was in this period that the fine stone-working craftsman began to reconstruct market towns and villages and what has come to be known as the Cotswold style evolved.

In 1644, when England was preoccupied with the Civil War and Royalist troops were stationed at Stow, Campden, Evesham and Pershore, all that is recorded about Snowshill is the entry in the tithe book that there were 360 sheep "sett upon Snowshill Hill". There is some evidence that there were troops in Stanton in a reference to broken church windows and it is thought that Cromwell's soldiers may have been responsible for damage to Broadway Court at the bottom of the hill. Despite the lack of positive documentary evidence, there is nevertheless every reason to suppose that Snowshill was looted during those turbulent and bloody times.

In 1649-50, a Parliamentary Survey of Church Livings was made which is now preserved in the Archiepiscopal Library at Lambeth Palace. The Commissioners' Return for "Staunton and Snowshill" reads:-

> We doe finde that mayntenance belonging to the Church of Staunton and the Chappell of Snowshill thereto annexed — that Staunton is worth eight and ffortie pounds per annum, and Snowshill ffortie pounds per annum, and that there is a present Minister, and that for both of them, about three score and fifteen families.[4]

It is interesting to note that, at the time of this survey, Cheltenham was only a stipendiary curacy worth forty pounds per annum, the same amount as Snowshill, and this valuation made it richer than many vicarages.

The accounts of the Rev. Thomas Vyner of 1658-59 provide a particularly interesting insight into the life and work of the villagers of Snowshill. The accounts refer to large quantities of woollen goods, mainly various types of stockings ranging in price from 2s. to 4s.6d. per pair. A parcel sold to Mr. Francis Dix on 3rd May 1659 included 967 pairs of stockings at a cost of £122.11s.5d.[5] It is, of course, well known that spinning and weaving were principal occupations of many Cotswold people but this emphasis on stockings is explained in Ogilby's road book, published in 1675, by the fact that Campden was a town famous for stockings. Apparently much Cotswold wool was only suitable for worsted stockings as it had become coarsened by rich feeding. It is this same road book that shows the White Way, running from Gloucester to Stratford-upon-Avon via Stanway, Snowshill and Chipping Campden, as one of the four principal roads through Gloucestershire. It would appear that the rector may have been acting as a sort of middle man between the stocking producers in Snowshill and Stanton and the buyers in Campden.

In the tithe book, an entry for 1697 gives a detailed account of the working of the tithe system. On 19th July the rector sold to John Smith the tithe hay of the Upper Meadow and Ram Close for the sum of £1.16s. He also sold the tithe hay of the Great and Little White Ox Leas to William Cook for £1.8s.; and to the Widow Turner (perhaps a forebear of the present Turner family in the village) he sold the tithe hay of the

22

common meadow and the other commonable places for 15s.: and the other tithe hay in "a place in the Hitching called Ten Horse-pastures" for 1s. Hitching is a Gloucestershire and Oxfordshire term for a ploughed and sown corner of a field otherwise lying fallow. The rector goes on to record a problem:-

> I began on Holy Rood Day to take up my tithe-milk of his cows that were fed in the wood-ground (Littleworth Wood) and I milked them without interruption till the 1st August when William Cook the tenant denied it me, affirming milk no longer tithable, upon which I made complaint to two Justices of the Peace, according to an Act of Parliament for the Recovery of Small Tithes, and they accordingly righted me, giving me five shillings for the milk he had detained, and afterwards I had no more trouble with him, but I gathered it so long as it was worth fetching, and that was after All Hallowtide, and with this milk I made above an Hundred of Cheese worth at the time £1.5s.[6]

It is not difficult to understand why the tithing system was regarded as so unsatisfactory and non-payment seems to have been a constantly recurring problem. In 1701 the Rev. Lionel Kirkham had difficulties with Henry Adams, a tenant farmer at Brockhampton which belonged to the Dowager Lady Coventry. In Easter week an agreement was reached whereby Adams should pay the rector money instead of tithes in kind. Instead of 18lb of wool, the sum of 9d. was to be paid. He was also to pay 3s.6d. for a calf and 18s.6d. for eight lambs. Furthermore, he still had to pay the very substantial sum of £10.8s.6d. for the preceding year's tithe of all his corn, which was still outstanding; "and for all his privy tithes, viz., hay, wool, lambs, milk, calves, colts, pigs, eggs, apples, garden and cottage £7." Adams was granted a lease by the rector of the privy tithes for three years at £7 a year, but the corn tithes were reserved to be gathered in kind. The rector adds that later in the year he gathered from Brockhampton in tithes:

Barley, 48 bushels
Oats,   40 bushels
Wheat, 2 thraves (1 thrave = 24 sheaves)
Pulse, "2 loads of which I suppose 12 bushels".[7]

In 1722 tithes at Brockhampton were again the subject of an agreement. On this occasion the agreement was between the rector and Richard Blackwell, the then tenant of Lord Coventry. In 1735, the Rev. Lionel Kirkham was still the rector, though in his declining years. Nevertheless he was planting trees at Snowshill. By now a certain Samuel Snow was the tenant farmer at Brockhampton and it was arranged that, subject to various conditions, his tithes should be commuted and that he should pay the rector £16 per annum in lieu.

The Manor under the Sambaches

In 1712, Snowshill Manor was bought by William Sambach, whose family had been in the village, as has been mentioned earlier, for some one hundred and fifty years at least. The Hockaday Abstracts record a marriage licence being granted in 1700 to "William Sambach of Snowshill, 32, bach. and Mary Ballard of Evesham, 22, maiden". It is not therefore surprising that William Sambach, and after him, his son William, were Lords of the Manor who had the interests of the village at heart. In about 1720, the Manor House went through its third and last main building period. The house was re-orientated to face South. This was done by the addition of a room on each floor at the Southern end with a pedimental doorway in the centre with the Sambach coat of arms above. No attempt was made for the new to blend with the old in style and the eighteenth century sash windows contrast strangely with the seventeenth century mullions. In 1723, William Sambach's son, William, aged "upwards of 20" married Anne Batson of St. Alban in Worcester, according to the Hockaday Abstracts, although Charles Wade believed her to have come from Bourton-on-the-Hill. On the death of his father he inherited the Manor but died aged forty without issue. Both father and son were buried in the chancel of the Church, near the altar, and a small marble monument to the son erected by his wife read that "he was a zealous friend of the Church with a true interest in his country".

Sir Robert Atkyns in "The Ancient and Present State of Gloucestershire", published in 1712 describes Snowshill manor as a "large house in the Place and a great Estate". This work also contains a bare description of the Church which was destroyed and rebuilt in the nineteenth century and of which little is known.

From Atkyns, it would appear that the Impropriation (i.e. the ownership of the advowson) was not always vested in the Lord of the Manor, which is more than reasonable since the Church is annexed to Stanton. Although at the time Atkyns wrote it was vested in Mr. Sambach and worth £40 yearly, "the Advowson of the Vicaridge of Snowshill was granted to William Rigg and Peter Gering 3 Mar. The advowson of the Church had been granted to John Eliot, who levied a Fine thereof to Thomas Dolman 5 Mar. John Dolman, son of Thomas, had livery thereof 15 Eliz." Atkyns tells us that, at the time of writing, the Glebe owned "One Yard Land, 12 Beast Pastures, 1 Horse Pasture and 400 Sheep Pastures." The question of the ownership of the advowson is clarified by Samuel Rudder in his "A New History of Gloucestershire", published in 1779, when he writes that "The Manor of Stanton, and the free chapel of Snowshill were granted by the Crown, 4 & 5 Phil. & Mar. to John Eliot, who obtained a licence to alienate them to Thomas Dolman the same year, and John Dolman, son of Thomas, had livery of the advowsons of this Church 15 Eliz."

Atkyns' population figures for Snowshill are interesting. He says in 1772 that there were 38 houses and about 192 inhabitants of whom 9 were freeholders. In 1984 there were approximately 150 inhabitants (139 being on the Electoral Roll) and approximately 60 households. In 1710 a household had an average of 5 members while in 1984 the average was 2.5 members. The annual birth rate in 1710 was 6 while the burial rate was 5. That Snowshill's population was steadily increasing at this time is borne out by the fact that Samuel Rudder wrote in 1779 "the number of families had increased to 48 and the number of inhabitants to 236".

William Sambach had died without an heir in 1743 and it appears that Snowshill Manor was inherited by his widow as it was not until 1759 that it was sold by auction at the George (now the Noel Arms) in Chipping Campden to Samuel Blackwell, who in 1762 through an Inclosure Act increased the acreage to 1223 acres, purchasing land from James Harrison, Thomas Shaylor and Thomas Breval. The Manor was described in the advertisement for the sale contained in the "Gloucester Journal" for Tuesday, January 9th, 1759, as being with an improvable estate and "situate in a very fine sporting country in the most agreeable part of the hills." The advertisement also said that the land was let at three hundred pounds per annum. Some of this was leased to Thomas Stanley, slat-digger, and his son Stephen. The Stanley family had been in the village since at least the beginning of the seventeenth century — a Stanley is mentioned in a roll dated 1604 and two Stanleys were buried in 1623 — and they were to remain as blacksmiths until the early part of the twentieth century.

Inclosure Act 1779

Inclosures in general caused hardship to the cottagers dependent on common land but there is no evidence that suffering was caused in Snowshill where the Lords of the Manor seem to have acted as good landlords, leasing cottages and small plots of land to village families, sometimes for a "quit-rent". Under the Inclosure Act, certain large common fields known as Rowden Field, Oat Hill Field, Thrustle-bridge, the Hitching and the field above the Hitching, consisting of about 500 acres, eighteen acres of Pasture "and also a large common Hill or Tract of waste Ground, called Snowshill Hill, containing by Estimation One thousand One hundred Acres or thereabouts" were inclosed. Samuel Blackwell, as Lord of the Manor was entitled to the Great and Small Tithes of Corn and Grain and the rector, the Rev. Robert Kirkham, received the advowson, certain glebe lands and the remaining third of the tithes except for the desmesne lands.

The landowners consisted of Samuel Blackwell and Robert Kirkham, together with Lord Sudeley "in the Kingdom of Ireland", the Hon. John Boscawen, James Harrison, clerk, Thomas Shaylor and Thomas Breval. Their houses and lands were inconveniently intermixed and dispersed giving rise to trespass and disputes among each other and their tenants. The landowners therefore desired that the land should be divided, allotted and inclosed to the advantage of all concerned. Commissioners from other villages were appointed to survey and set out the land. Samuel Blackwell and his heirs received an allotment over and above their own lands as compensation for tithes previously received. Robert Kirkham and his successors also received an allotment in compensation for loss of glebe land and right of common and a further allotment in lieu of tithes from old houses, cottages, orchards and ancient inclosures. Thus under the Inclosure Act both Right of Common and tithes were removed, although the Lord of the Manor's manorial rights remained untouched.

Shortly after the Inclosure Act, in 1779, the Manor was bought by John Small of Clapham, who was the first of a series of absentee landlords who owned Snowshill Manor until 1919 when it was bought and restored by Charles Paget Wade. During the intervening period of nearly one hundred and fifty years the Manor House was used as a farmhouse and entered into a long period of decline.

The Nineteenth Century

In the first decade of the century the two main properties, Snowshill Manor and Snowshill Farm, both changed hands but since only absentee landlords were involved, these changes are unlikely to have made much impact on the life of the village.

Snowshill Manor

Charles Wade, possibly an ancestor of Charles Paget Wade, is thought to have lived at Snowshill Manor at the end of the eighteenth century and H. Price and Edward Forster had some interest in the property around that time but by 1803, the Manor had been inherited by John Small's grand-daughter, Mrs. Ponton. By 1832, the Manor had passed to Mrs. Ponton's son, Thomas, who was known locally as "Ponto" although his visits to the village were rare.

The Reverend F. E. Witts records in his diary that Charles Marshall was living at Snowshill in 1825 and that he was also Lord Wemyss' steward. Eleven years later there is another entry in Witts' diary in which he refers to Lord Wemyss' pleasure in the way in which Mr. Marshall managed his estate at Stanway.[1] Charles Marshall appears to have held a lease on the entire Manor of Snowshill until 1853, the year in which Francis Woodgate bought the estate. In the same year John Marshall took a separate lease of Snowshill Hill which consisted of 468 acres for £225 per annum. He had been at Snowshill Hill since at least 1851, when the census records that he employed nineteen labourers. Charles Marshall, remained as tenant of the Manor and Manor Farm but died the following year, aged seventy-nine, leaving his widow, Susanna, and one of his daughters as tenants of the Manor and the 759 acres of Manor Farm for which they paid Francis Woodgate a rent of £550 per annum. Charles Marshall's son, also called Charles, was at Stanton Court at this time but died two months before his father, at the age of fifty-six, and was buried in the Marshall family grave at Snowshill. Susanna Marshall died in 1858, aged eighty.

In 1919, Charles Wade was told a ghost story by Richard Dark concerning an event which was said to have occurred after Charles Marshall's death. There is some conflict of evidence as to the exact date but it must have it occurred some time before 1858 because Mrs. Marshall is one of the principal people supposedly involved. The story runs that one of Mrs. Marshall's labourers, a certain Richard Carter, father-in-law of Richard Dark, was returning home from Hill Barn Farm one night when he saw the ghost of his former employer, Charles

Marshall, riding alongside him on a black horse. This happened on several occasions and, in the end, Carter sought the advice of the rector who advised him to confront the ghost with the words, "What troublest thou, in the name of the Lord?" This he did and thereupon the ghost told Carter to meet him at midnight at the chaff house. Carter did as he was told and was given a secret message to convey to Mrs. Marshall. The contents of the message were never divulged but it was assumed to reveal the location of hidden money.

Francis Woodgate, who bought the Manor in 1853 had only a brief period of ownership as he died on the 14th February 1856 and left the estate to his son, also called Francis. Francis Woodgate junior, being a young lieutenant in the Life Guards and apparently in need of substantial sums of ready money, mortgaged the estate as soon as he inherited it. The mortgage contained complicated provisions for redemption which the unfortunate lieutenant failed to meet and, after a final money-raising exercise in 1859, he was forced to sell the Manor in 1860. On the 1st August of that year the estate, then consisting of 1226 acres, was sold to John, William and James Sidebottom, cotton spinners, of Glossop and owners of a number of other estates. The indenture of sale states that the tenancy of Manor Farm, which, of course, included the Manor House and which Mrs. Marshall and one of her daughters had held after Charles Marshall's death, was then held by two Misses Marshall. The indenture unfortunately contains two blank spaces where their Christian names should have been.

The Schedule to this 1860 indenture gives a very good picture of the land comprising the estate at the time and lists the various fields and other land by name or description. (The Schedule is set out in full in Appendix V.)

It is not clear at what stage the lease to the two Misses Marshall to which the indenture refers actually came to an end nor is it clear in what capacity the subsequent tenants, the Cooks, had been "in occupation for several years" but, in 1860, the Sidebottoms leased Manor Farm and 759 acres to Charles Cook, the younger, "of Snowshill" and Charles Cook the elder of Toddington. As this lease refers to the Cooks having been in "occupation" for several years rather than using any other term, their rights must, at best, have been those of sub-tenants as it is quite clear that the two Misses Marshall were the tenants of Manor Farm at the time Woodgate junior sold to the Sidebottoms.

One of the Miss Marshalls must also have been remembered with gratitude as she set up one of the two village charities. Her charity produced nine pounds a year to buy coal for the poor. The other charity had been set up in 1849 by the Honourable Anne Rushout of Blockley Park who gave two hundred pounds each to Blockley, Pebworth, Willersey and Snowshill. After suffering a ten per cent government levy to which it was unfortunately subject, this yielded five pounds per annum to purchase blankets for the poor chosen from those who were not receiving parochial relief. These blankets were distributed by the rector and churchwardens at Christmas and, in later years, it is recalled that this had a marked and beneficial effect on the level of church attendance on Christmas Day.

No fewer than nine members of the Marshall family are commemorated in the stained glass windows which adorn St. Barnabas Church which was built in 1864. It is questionable whether all of the nine actually lived in the village.

The lease which the Cooks took in 1860 was for twelve years at £840 per annum. This high rent reflects the fact that the 1860s were the golden age of nineteenth century farming, although the seeds of the downward trend were soon to become apparent. The lease contained various clauses including the requirement for crops to be rotated and manure to be used. Grass was only to be mown once a year and not later than the 5th August. Wood and ironwork was to be painted at least twice with oil plant.

In 1892 the Cooks' lease was renewed for a further five years but at a drastically reduced rent of only £300 per annum. Agriculture was by now in a state of great depression. Cereal prices had collapsed in the 1870s and wool prices followed suit in the 1880s. Rising imports of agricultural commodities and several drought years were particularly to blame. The 1892 lease contained a number of strict clauses, among which were that the landlords retained timber, shooting and fishing rights. At the end of the agreement, the interior of the cottages were to be painted with two coats of best quality paint. Hedges were to be lay cut and no trees were to be lopped or cut. No new footpaths were to be established and eight horses were to be stabled to produce manure. It was probably at the expiry of this lease in 1897 that Charles Lovesey took over as tenant of the Manor House, farm and 214 acres.

Snowshill Hill had a number of occupants during the Sidebottoms' ownership. John Marshall died in November 1867 and in his will, he directed his executors to surrender the lease of Snowshill Hill which was duly done in September 1868. The Sidebottoms then leased the farm for £450 per annum to John Hyatt, who in 1874 assigned the lease to Joseph Holtham, who also held another lease from the Sidebottoms for land in Honeybourne.

By 1882 the great agricultural depression was causing problems to landowners and often desperate hardship to tenant farmers. The Sidebottoms wanted Mr. Holtham to remain at Snowshill Hill but he was unwilling to do so. Snowshill Hill Farm, the Residence and 450 acres, was widely advertised but to no avail and in September of that year the Sidebottoms leased the property to Martin Thomas Meadows, then of Hornsleasow, at a reduced rent of £285 per annum. The Sidebottoms were only prepared to offer a three year lease as the rent was so low but, as they said to their solicitor, "we hope you will come to terms with Mr. Meadows as we don't wish the farm thrown on our hands". However, in those hard times, Mr. Meadows still had problems in paying the rent and in January 1883 the Sidebottoms' agent wrote to their solicitors in Evesham refusing to pay for repairs to Snowshill Hill until the rent had been paid. There is an interesting bill for the same year written by the agent, for artificial manure.

Snowshill Farm and the Hyatts

There were three main farms in Snowshill, Manor Farm and Snowshill Hill, which together formed the estate of the Manor, and a third, Snowshill Farm, which at the beginning of the nineteenth century contained 508 acres but which grew to 900 acres by 1851.

In 1779, the Hon. Richard Gore, stated to be living in "the Kingdom of Ireland" had leased the "messuage, tenement and farm lying and being in Snowshill previously occupied by Thomas Hyatt" and also "the cottage adjoining the farmyard in the occupation of Robert Pain" to William Hyatt, son of Thomas, and William's son, also called Thomas, for twenty-one years at a yearly rent of £275. In 1803 William Hyatt died and the lease was taken over by his son, Thomas. On the 3rd September, 1808, the following advertisement appeared in the "Morning Chronicle" of London:-

> Compact Farm, near Broadway, freehold and tithe-free to be sold by Private Contract, a compact and highly improvable freehold farm called Snowshill Farm, in the parish of Snowshill, in the County of Gloucester, now in the occupation of Mr. Hyatt; containing upwards of 508 acres, including 30 acres of woodland, and well planted, lying within a ring fence, and in a high state of cultivation, with a substantial farm-house and commodious building. Also a detached Cottage and Garden in the village of Snowshill.

It is not known who bought Snowshill Farm then but at some stage the property came into the ownership of Lord Redesdale who owned Batsford and many thousands of acres of Cotswold countryside. Redesdale inherited the Gloucestershire estates from his uncle by marriage, Thomas Freeman, in 1808 and it is not impossible that he sought to add to his inheritance by the purchase of Snowshill Farm.

It was however not the Redesdales, but the Hyatt family who were to make their mark and play a leading role in the life of the village and the estate remained in the occupation of the Hyatts until well into the twentieth century. Another branch of the Hyatt family leased Brockhampton Farm from the Hon. John Coventry.

On the night of the 29th February, 1832, a Highway Robbery occurred in which "two men stopped Thomas Hyatt of Snowshill, in the County of Gloucester, Farmer, on his way home from Tewkesbury market, and within 300 yards of his own house, who after knocking him down and inflicting several severe wounds on his head and face, robbed him of all the money which he had in his pockets. They also took from his person a silver hunting watch, No. 8655, a memorandum book, wherein he kept his Banking Account with Messrs. Lachmere, Wall & Isaac, Old Bank, Tewkesbury." A reward of £50 was offered by Hyatt in addition to another reward which would be paid by "the Bourne Association" for any information leading to conviction. The Bourne Association was one of the voluntary groups or associations called "Societies for the Prosecution of Felons" formed by the gentry and well-to-do farmers in an attempt to protect their property and bring wrong-doers to court. We do not know whether the robbers were caught but the description of the episode and the fact that Mr. Hyatt could call upon the assistance of the Bourne Association demonstrates that he was a man of some substance.

George Diston recalls that Thomas Hyatt had had a stone in the dry stone wall carved to commemorate the spot where he was robbed in the lane to Brockhampton. It was known as the "Robbery Stone" and the Hyatts always ensured that it was kept clear of overgrowth. Unfortunately it is no longer kept clear and the writer has been unable to find it.

By 1851, according to the census of that year, Thomas Hyatt was farming 900 acres, making Snowshill Farm the largest single farm in the parish. He employed thirty-five labourers at that time.

In 1852 Thomas Hyatt was Surveyor of Highways for the Parish of Snowshill and was responsible for the collection of Highway Rates. Liability to pay rates had existed since the Poor Relief Act of 1601 and although the Poor Rate continued as the principal rate for more than two centuries, various other rates were also levied under separate enactments and full consolidation did not occur until 1925 when the Office of Overseer of the Poor was abolished. The Snowshill Highway Rate in 1852 was 3d in the pound. The following are some extracts from the account which Thomas Hyatt rendered to the Justices in Winchcombe for that year:-

	Annual Value	Rate	Property
Thomas Hyatt	£297- 0- 0	£3- 0- 0	Snowshill Farm
Richard Kilby	150-12- 0	1-17- 8	Brockhampton
J & M Meadows	123-10- 0	1-10-10½	Smallthorns
Charles Marshall	454- 0- 0	5-13- 6	Manor Farm
John Marshall	286-15- 0	3-11- 8	Snowshill Hill

and an example from the other end of the scale:-

John Stanley	£2-16- 0	8½d	The Forge

Highway Robbery.

£50 REWARD

ON Wednesday Night the 29th of February last, about Twelve o'clock. Two Men stopped THOMAS HYATT, of Snowshill, in the County of Gloucester, Farmer, on his way home from Tewkesbury Market, and within 300 yards of his own House, who after knocking him down and inflicting several severe wounds upon his Head and Face, robbed him of all the Money which he had in his Pockets. They also took from his Person a SILVER HUNTING WATCH, "No. 8655;" a Memorandum Book, with red covers, and also another Book, wherein he kept his Banking Account with Messrs. LECHMERE, WALL, and ISAAC, Old Bank, Tewkesbury.

One of the Robbers, who wore a long Brown Coat, was a little taller and stouter than his Companion.

Whoever will give information, upon which the Perpetrators can be Convicted, shall receive a Reward of £.50 (over and above the Reward which will be paid by "the Bourne Association,") from me,

Snowshill, 3d March, 1832.

THOMAS HYATT.

George May, Printer and Bookseller, Evesham.

By 1864, both annual values and the rate in the pound had materially increased. The annual value of the Forge, described as "a cottage, garden and blacksmith's shop", had risen, for example, to £3-10-0. Hyatt's ledger for that year, the last for which he made entries, shows that both a penny rate and a ninepenny rate were levied, the rate having been raised to sixpence in 1862. The total rate collected by Mr. Hyatt rose from £19-16-2½ in 1852 to £79-18-3½ in 1864 when the overall value of the parish was £2131-0-0.

On the 27th March, 1857, George Hyatt was appointed Parish Constable for Snowshill by the Justices sitting in Winchcombe. The office of constable had existed since the thirteenth century and, prior to the creation of a regular police force, it was the constable who was responsible for law and order in his own parish. In earlier times he was appointed by the Manor Courts, but with their decline in the seventeenth and eighteenth centuries it often became necessary for the parish Vestry or the Justices of the Peace to appoint. By the early nineteenth century the job of Parish Constable, which was unpaid, had become generally unpopular and where the lot fell to someone of substance, he frequently paid someone else to do it. Under the Parish Constables Act of 1842, any able-bodied resident of the parish, aged between twenty-five and fifty-five, who was rated on tenements of a net yearly value of £4 or upwards was liable to serve as Parish Constable unless he could show that he came within one of the specified exemptions. The office had probably never been a particularly onerous task in Snowshill which was fortunate in being remote from the unrest which had been experienced earlier in the South of the county with riots over bread prices and the Swing riots in which farm labourers protested against the introduction of threshing machines. Although the 1842 Act was not finally repealed until 1964, by the time of George Hyatt's appointment the office was well on the way to becoming an anachronism because Gloucestershire magistrates were among the first in the country to take advantage of the provisions of the County Police Act of 1839 which enabled police forces to be established outside London and, by 1857, the county police were comparatively well established.

Snowshill Farm continued to be occupied by successive members of the Hyatt family until 1914.

Brockhampton

In 1812 the Hon. John Coventry leased Brockhampton Farm, which consisted of 213 acres, to William Hyatt for £250 for the first year and £350 thereafter. John Coventry sold Brockhampton and Middle Hill to the great bibliophile Sir Thomas Phillipps Bt. in 1825. Phillipps made his home at Middle Hill and these lands remained in Phillipps ownership until 1916. In 1850, however, Hyatt received notice that he was no longer required to pay rent to Sir Thomas but to others who had become joint Lords of the Manor of Brockhampton. A likely explanation of this comes from the diary of the Rev. F. E. Witts of Upper Slaughter who, in his entry for 28th June 1828, refers to Phillipps' non-payment of mortgage interest being likely to be pursued at law. He added that Sir Thomas persisted in his old expensive taste of book and manuscript collecting. It would appear that he did not learn the error of his ways.

St. Barnabas Church 1864

Very little is known of the old church at Snowshill and even its dedication is uncertain though village tradition believes that it was to St. George. This is supported, but not proved, by the fact that it is marked as St. George's Church on the Ordnance Survey map of 1884, which is in any event wrong as St. Barnabas Church had already been there for twenty years. We may, however, be reasonably sure that the old church was not dedicated to St. Barnabas as this is a typically Victorian dedication and one not normally found in ancient churches. Sadly no picture has yet come to light of the old church and we have just two scant eighteenth century descriptions. The first comes from Dr. Parsons who was Chancellor of the Diocese of Gloucester for thirty-four years. He wrote, "the Church and chancell are but small and at ye West there is a stone tower with two bells".[3] Sir Robert Atkyns in his "The Ancient and Present State of Gloucestershire" of 1712 wrote, "the Church is small, and hath a Towere at the West end adorned with Battlements and Pinnacles".

What befell this Church is unknown. Opinion seems divided as to whether it burnt down or collapsed. Neglect of the fabric of rural churches was not uncommon in the eighteenth and early nineteenth centuries. For example, it was for this reason that the church in nearby Childswickham needed to be almost completely rebuilt in 1870 and the likelihood is that the same circumstances prevailed in Snowshill. The faculty for the building of St. Barnabas is dated 24th June 1863 but the name of the architect is unknown. There is a record in "The Church Builder" for 1865 that the Church cost £1700 to build. It is known that no grant was received from the Incorporated Church Building Society but there is no record of who paid the bill. It is known that it had been intended that the new Church should have a spire but it would appear that promised funds were not forthcoming and in the end it was found necessary to build a low pointed roof on the tower as a temporary measure. Strangely there seem to be no diocesan records about the Church and no report in the "Evesham Journal" about its consecration. It would appear that it was built entirely from new materials except for the three objects of antiquity it contains. We do not, however, know whether these three objects were rescued from the old Church or whether they came from somewhere else. If it were known that they came from the old Church, then it would largely disprove any theory that it burnt down. The bell, one and not two as in the previous Church, was cast in Bristol between 1350 and 1380. It is distinguished by the use of a cross and also bears the impression of a coin. It is inscribed with the words "+ In Name of Trinite Gilis Belle Men Calle Me".[4] The bell was rehung with new fittings in February, 1963, by John Taylor & Co. of Loughborough. The font, which now has an oak cover in memory of John Hands, clerk of the parish for nearly fifty years, is fifteenth century and the pulpit is Jacobean, c1640.

All the stained glass windows are in memory of the Marshall family. The East window, designed by Ward and Hughes, which portrays the appearance of Mary Magdalene, the Crucifixion and the Ascension, was installed in 1864 when the Church was built. It commemorates:-

Charles Marshall — died March 1st 1854 aged 56
Russell William Richard Marshall — died January 25th
    1844 aged 36
Charles Marshall — died May 8th 1854 aged 79
Susanna Mary Marshall — died August 31st 1858 aged 80

The other windows came later. The North ones are in memory of Letitia Dyrham Marshall, who died September 18th 1867 (the window portraying St. Luke), and Lucretia Marshall, who died February 8th 1849 (St. Matthew), and the South windows commemorate another Lucretia, who died April 16th 1867 (St. Mark) and John Marshall, who died November 10th 1867 (St. John). Frances Portal gave the West window, which represents Jesus at the Well of Sychar and Jesus at the House of Martha and Mary, in memory of her sister, Elizabeth Ann Marshall, 1823-1885.

The National School

The Education Acts of the eighteen-seventies were not popular in rural communities where boys started to work at the age of about ten and girls went into service, both providing a welcome supplement to the family income. The high rate of illiteracy is clearly reflected in the Marriage Register for the period from 1770-1812. Out of thirty-eight marriages solemnised in Snowshill during this period, in thirty-six cases either the bride or groom, and generally both, were unable to sign the register other than by a cross. When the National School was built in 1871, therefore, it met a very real need. It was built to cater for sixty-five children but the subsequent average attendance was forty-five. Interestingly, the average school attendance at the much larger village of Broadway in 1866 was only one hundred and twelve.

The New Road to Broadway

Snowshill probably owes its original existence largely to the fact that it lay near the crossing of prehistoric trackways and the narrow winding lane between Snowshill and Campden was part of one of the most important roads in Gloucestershire when Ogilby compiled the first usable road book in 1675. These routes greatly diminished in importance and the way to Broadway was more often than not impassable in winter. This was a rough track called Coneygree Lane which wound its way down the hill via Kites Nest, coming out into the present Snowshill Road at Middle Hill drive. Although it is believed that Coneygree Lane at one time formed part of the road from Oxford to Worcester, Snowshill must indeed have become a remote and inaccessable place, particularly in winter. It was a major event, therefore, in the history of Snowshill when a meeting was held in the Broadway Vestry Room on the 13th December, 1872, to consider the proposal made by Mr. Morris and Mr. Hensley that a new public road should be constructed between Broadway Old Church and Snowshill Village, a distance of 2450 yards. Charles Cook and George Hyatt attended the meeting representing Snowshill. The proposal that such a road was desirable was carried unanimously. All the owners of the land through which the new road was to pass gave their consent and the final decision to construct was taken on the 7th August, 1873. The cost was estimated to be eight hundred and fourteen pounds, six hundred pounds of which had already been promised. The road was completed in August 1877, although the cost by then had risen to £881.9.8. due, it was said, to the late very wet season.

NEW PUBLIC ROAD

FROM SNOWSHILL TO BROADWAY.

The Committee appointed to carry out the above work, beg to report its completion, and to submit to the Subscribers a Statement of Accounts, from which it will be seen that the total cost of the road has been £881 9s. 8d.; towards which donations to the amount of £665 7s. 8d. have been promised, leaving a deficiency of £216 2s. 0d.

In addition to the above expenditure, gratuitous hauling to the amount of nearly £200 has been done by occupiers of land in the immediate neighbourhood.

The original estimated cost was £814; its excess was caused by extra material, rendered necessary by the late very wet season.

The Committee appeal to all owners and occupiers of property and residents in the neighbourhood for assistance to pay of the existing debt, as the road will be a great public benefit, and open a much shorter and more direct route from hill to vale.

Donations will be gladly received and further information given by the undersigned

GEORGE HYATT, Snowshill, *Treasurer.*
CHARLES COOK, JUNR., Snowshill, *Secretary.*

August, 1877.

TREASURER'S ACCOUNT.

Receipts.	£	s.	d.	Expenditure.	£	s.	d.
Donations as per List	652	2	0	Mr. F. P. Webb, for making the road	650	0	0
Interest	13	5	8	Mr. Hensley, for plans, &c.	14	0	0
				Mr. Griffith's solicitor's bill	9	19	0
£	665	7	8	Messrs. Gill & Co., for walling	13	17	11
				Mess.s Figgett & Co, labourer's work	9	16	6
				Messrs. Cole & Wood for Quick	37	6	0
Amount required to clear off debt	216	2	0	Messrs. Ainge, &c., planting Quick	18	6	0
				Messrs. Vizzard & Turner for fencing	98	4	3
				Estimated cost of keeping the road in repair for 12 months after completion	30	0	0
Total £	881	9	8	Total £	881	9	8

Subscribers to the new public road from Snowshill to Broadway

DONATIONS.

	£	s.	d.
The Messrs. Sidebottom	150	0	0
The Earl of Wemyss	75	0	0
The Earl of Redesdale	75	0	0
Mr. Charles Cook, jun	50	0	0
Mr. George Hyatt	50	0	0
Mr. Wilson	39	0	0
Messrs. Morris	20	0	0
The Earl Beauchamp	10	0	0
Lord Northwick	10	0	0
Mr. Charles Cook	10	0	0
Mr. C. Burrows	10	0	0
Miss Talbot	5	5	0
Mr. H. W. Smith	5	5	0
Mr. Wynniatt	5	0	0
Mr. Averill	5	0	0
Mr. Chadwick	5	0	0
Mr. B. Burrows	5	0	0
Mr. W. W. Brown	5	0	0
Mr. T. Cook	5	0	0
A Friend	5	0	0
Miss Marshall	5	0	0
Miss E. Marshall	5	0	0
Mr. C. Phillipps	5	0	0
Mr. J. Hyatt	5	0	0
The Earl of Coventry	3	3	0
Rev. W. H. Bloxham	3	3	0
Messrs. New, Prance, and Garrard	2	2	0
Miss Phillipps	2	2	0
Mr. G. Phillipps	2	2	0
Mr. J. Phillipps	2	2	0
Rev. G. D. Bourne	2	0	0
Mr. E. S. Lurrows	2	0	0
Mr. J. P. Dunn	2	0	0
Messrs. Webb and Co.	2	0	0
Mr. E. L. Foss	1	1	0
Mr. Foxlow	1	1	0
Mr. E. Webb	1	1	0
The Hon. J. Hewitt	1	0	0
Mr. Arkell	1	0	0
Mr. J. Ashmore	1	0	0
Mrs. Averill	1	0	0
Mr. Arkell	1	0	0
Mr. G. Burrows	1	0	0
Mr. W. Byrd	1	0	0
Mr. Coates	1	0	0
Mr. Coldicott	1	0	0
Mr. W. Coldicott	1	0	0
Mr. R. Coldicott	1	0	0
Mrs. C. Cook	1	0	0
Mr. J. Cook	1	0	0
Messrs. Chidley and Collins	1	0	0
Mr. Clark	1	0	0
Mr. Griffiths	1	0	0
Carried over	**£606**	**7**	**0**

	£	s.	d.
Brought over	606	7	0
Mrs Dutton	1	0	0
Mr. Eades	1	0	0
Mr. Gibbs	1	0	0
Mr. R. Green	1	0	0
Mrs. Griffin	1	0	0
Mrs. J. Hyatt	1	0	0
Mr. B. T. Hyatt	1	0	0
Mr. Horne	1	0	0
Mr. James	1	0	0
Mr. Jackson	1	0	0
Mr. James	1	0	0
Mr. Kilby	1	0	0
Mr. O. J. Morris	1	0	0
Mr. J. N. Moore	1	0	0
Mr. C. Morris	1	0	0
Mr. Mould	1	0	0
Mr. Randell	1	0	0
Mr. A. Richardson	1	0	0
Mr. Rimell	1	0	0
Mr. W. Rimell	1	0	0
Mr. A. Roberts	1	0	0
Mr. Robinson	1	0	0
Mr. H. Smith	1	0	0
Mr Rushout	1	0	0
Mr. F. Stanley	1	0	0
Mr. H Stanley	1	0	0
Mr. E. Stayt	1	0	0
Mr. G. Stayt	1	0	0
Mr. H. Stayt	1	0	0
Mr. W. Taylor	1	0	0
Mr. G. Taylor	1	0	0
Mr. C. Turner	1	0	0
Mr. H Overbury	1	0	0
Mrs. Wilson	1	0	0
Mr. Warmington	1	0	0
Mr. J. Walker	1	0	0
Mr. H. Workman	1	0	0
Rev. F. B. Witts	1	0	0
Mr. Walker	1	0	0
Mr. Wright	1	0	0
Mr Butler	0	10	0
Mr Dadge	0	10	0
Mr. S. Hemming	0	10	0
Mr. Holder	0	10	0
Mr. Kingsett	0	10	0
Mr. C. W. Morris	0	10	0
Mr. J Morris	0	10	0
Mr. A. Morris	0	10	0
Mr. G. Roberts	0	10	0
Mr. H. Smith	0	10	0
Mr. J. Stanley	0	10	0
Mr Cole	0	5	0
Total	**£652**	**2**	**0**

Reproduced by kind permission of the Gloucestershire Record Office[6]

1   *Snowshill c1900*

2   *St. Barnabas Church c1890*

3   *Village group c1902*

4   *Walter Turner outside Ivy Cottage c1910*

5   *Village from Oat Hill c1905*

6   *Village from Oat Hill 1986*

7   *Snowshill Manor c1910*

8   *Snowshill Manor 1986*

9   *Manor Cottages c1900*

10   *Manor Cottages 1986*

11   *Snowshill village c1934*
(Mrs. Nancy Turner in foreground)

12   *Snowshill 1986*

13   *Wimbledon Scouts outside E. W. Turner's shop in late 1920's*

14   *Snowshill Post Office c1932*

15   *Snowshill Arms c1898*

16   *Snowshill Arms c1929*

17   *Cricket team 1921*
Back row: Dick Wilkes, Jim Aston, Joe Gardener, Bill Diston, George Diston.
Front row: Archie Turner, Ralph Keyte, Major Milvain, Frank Turner, Freddie
Chandler, Jimmy Hull.

18   *Snowshill Mummers c1936*
(Walter Turner, Bernard Smith, Reg Turner, Jack Smith, 'Nurk' Meadows,
Bill Meadows, Bill Smith).

19

School photograph 1928
Back row: Ruby Diston, Phyllis Wilkes, Owen Basford, Charlie Smith, unknown,
Jim Corbett, Bill Turner, Margaret Spires, Rosie James.
Front row: Eileen Turner, Nancy Meadows, Beat Turner, Bill Meadows, Eddie
Russell, Agnes Holmes, Iris Diston, Brenda Basford.

20

A working team c1900

Village Life

In all the records for Snowshill in the nineteenth century, three names stand out, Turner, Stanley and Diston, and there are also a number of references to Corbett. The Stanleys left the village in the nineteen-twenties and Leslie Diston died in 1985. Happily, the Turner and the Corbett families are still well represented and the National Trust has recently commemorated the long association of the Diston family with the village by naming Leslie Diston's cottage "Diston's Cottage". It is to join other cottages which the National Trust owns in the row in being available for holiday-makers. Perhaps the more enquiring will learn something of the part played by the Diston family in the village through the centuries.

In 1842, Charles Keyte, or Schemer Keyte as he was known, a relation of the Turner family, brought fame to himself and the village, with his invention of what is believed to be one of the earliest sewing machines. The model is now housed in the textile section of the Science Museum in London. He was born in Ivy Cottage but later moved to what is now called Rose Cottage and it was there that he designed his machine.

In the Hockaday Abstracts there is an entry for 1812 for an application to the Bishop of Gloucester by Stephen Stanley, Mary Stanley, David Taylor and Elizabeth Brain for permission to use a building belonging to Stephen Stanley, a labourer, as a place of worship by Protestant dissenters. The permission was granted and then it was later renewed in 1841. It would be interesting to know how many non-conformists, and of what denomination, there were in the village in addition to those listed. At least one of the Stanleys, James Stanley, must have been regarded as part of the establishment around this time, although perhaps not one of the most popular members, as he is mentioned in the indenture of sale of the Snowshill Arms in 1836 as being "an Officer of Excise".

The 1851 census gives some insight into life in the village at the time. The population had increased from 236 in 1801 to a peak of 303 in 1851. In the area including Snowshill Hill, Smallthorns and Brockhampton, there were 59 inhabited houses and 61 separate occupiers.

In 1851 the Turner family included David Turner and his family, Edwin Turner the wheelwright, then aged 19, James Turner, a carpenter, John Turner aged 77 and Charles Turner, a gardener. Charles Keyte, presumably Schemer Keyte, was Charles Turner's son-in-law and there was also Thomas Keyte, a stone mason and his three sons, John, William and Edward, the last described as "a scholar" aged seven.

Stephen Stanley, the non-conformist was now aged 77 and is sadly described as a "pauper and agricultural labourer". One would hope that the smithy was doing good business as John Stanley, aged 55 and two of his three sons are listed as blacksmiths. The youngest, Charles, destined to be the last blacksmith in the village was then aged eleven.

The Distons were represented by Mary, aged 70 and described as an agricultural labourer, and Richard. There were two Corbett households, William Corbett aged 71 and his son William aged 28 and James Corbett aged 39 and his three young sons, William, Charles and Henry.

In addition to these familiar Snowshill names, there are other entries of interest in the 1851 census. The Rev. Henry Robert "curate not having the cure of souls" had no fewer than five servants, while Elizabeth Smith, aged 70 and an annuitant, had one servant. There was also a grocer in the village, William Woodward and his daughter Ann, who was a dressmaker.

Elizabeth Troughton, aged 61, was a silk dresser and she has the melancholy distinction of being the only person in Snowshill to make news in the "Evesham Journal" during the first eight years of its publications. On the 18th November, 1865, the following appeared:-

SUICIDE AT SNOWSHILL

On Saturday last a distressing case of suicide occurred at the above village. It appears an old woman named Elizabeth Troughton committed suicide by strangling herself with her apron strings. The unfortunate woman (through the blindness of her husband) has lately been in a very low desponding way fearing that on account of her husband's affliction, they would become so reduced that ultimately she should be sent to the Union.

Rural life in the nineteenth century has been greatly romanticised both in the popular imagination and in novels as some mythical golden age. Historical evidence, however, suggests that the reality, particularly in the Southern half of England, was very different. The life of the agricultural labourer was very hard, beset by poverty, poor housing, high infant mortality, poor nutrition and consequent poor health. The reference to 'hovels' in the schedule to the indenture of 13th August 1860, which is set out in Appendix V, and the frequent references to 'paupers' in the 1851 census would indicate that Snowshill was no exception to this pattern.

On the 29th September, 1836, Anthony Beard bought the Snowshill Arms, then described as a malthouse, from Edward Skey who was a maltser and who had owned the property since the beginning of the century. In the 1851 census, the Beards were listed as cordwainers,

Anthony being a master cordwainer and his sons being journeymen cordwainers. That Anthony Beard's principal occupation should have been that of a cordwainer, or, in the more modern wording of Kelly's Directory of 1870, a shoemaker, is understandable. Being a publican in a small village at that time would only have been a part-time job and shoemaking, or, more precisely, bootmaking, was an important trade in an agricultural community before the days of the rubber wellington boot. An agricultural labourer would hope to be able to afford a new pair of boots each year, usually bought after the harvest. At other times of the year, the shoemaker would have to rely mainly on shoe and harness repairs for his living so shoemaking and beer retailing were two trades which could be combined readily.

Anthony Beard died on the 21st May, 1871, and left the Snowshill Arms to his only legitimate son, John, who in Kelly's Directory of 1876 was described only as a shoemaker notwithstanding the fact that he was clearly running the pub as well. However, in 1879, he is listed as "shoemaker and beer retailer". John Beard died a bachelor and intestate on the 29th November, 1884, and Letters of Administration were granted to his natural brother, William, who as his only next-of-kin, became entitled to his property. William Beard in turn died on the 5th January, 1893 leaving the Snowshill Arms to his two sons, Anthony Edwin Beard and Edwin Beard.

There is a photograph of the Snowshill Arms, taken around 1890, which shows William Beard as publican on an inn sign fixed to the East wall of the property. This photograph is particularly interesting as it shows the building as less than half its present size with the entrance at the South-West side. The building, as seen in this photograph, which now forms the North-East wing of the present pub, is believed to be one of the oldest buildings in the village, probably contemporary with the early parts of the Manor, and the beams are thought to be original. Until the early nineteen hundreds, beer was brewed in the brew house attached to the main building and in the late nineteenth century Donnington Brewery supplied hops and malt for the purpose.

At the time of their father's death, neither of the Beard brothers lived in the village. Anthony Edwin was a butcher in Guiting Power and his brother, Edwin, was a schoolmaster at Bednall in Staffordshire. On the 11th September, 1893, Anthony Edwin sold his half share in the Snowshill Arms to Edwin, father of Blanche Ada Beard, for £235 and he ran the pub until he died in 1911.

By 1870, Kelly lists Richard Woodward as having taken over the grocery shop. By then there was a second shop in the village and this was run by Mrs. Ann Hemming. The 1870 Kelly tells us that the population in 1861 was 235. This would have been such a sharp decline that it is almost certainly an error, especially because in 1879, again according to

41

Kelly, the figure was 260, which seems in line with the general trend for a small agricultural community at this time. Miss Emily White was Snowshill's schoolmistress but, by 1885, Miss Jesse Rowley had taken over and Jane Hemming and David Smith ran the shops. Charles Stanley had taken over the smithy from his brother John and John Hands was the parish clerk. Despite the lack of a Post Office, the postal service was excellent with letters being collected each day at 5.00 pm from the wall letter box opposite the Manor gate. In 1887 the collection was at 4.45 pm but letters continued to arrive at 8.30 each morning.

By 1901, the population of the village had dropped sharply during the preceding twenty years to 214 and the rateable value of the parish had declined from £2146 in 1876 to £1106 in 1897. The agricultural depression was undoubtedly the principal cause of both these changes.

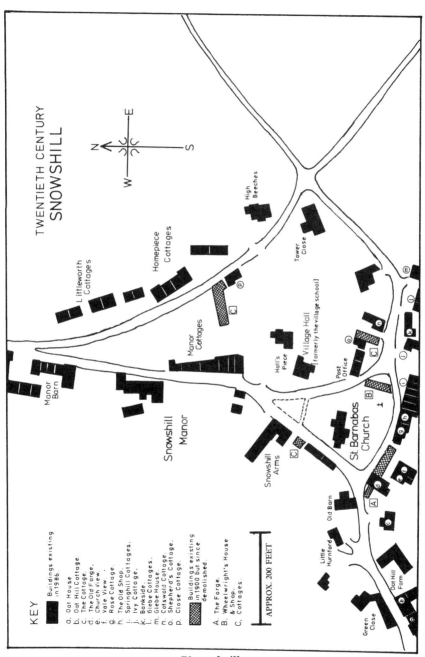

KEY

■ Buildings existing in 1986.

a. Oat House
b. Oat Hill Cottage.
c. The Cottage.
d. The Old Forge.
e. Church View.
f. Vale View.
g. Rose Cottage.
h. The Old Shop.
i. Springhill Cottages.
j. Ivy Cottage.
k. Bankside.
l. Glebe Cottages.
m. Glebe House.
n. Cotswold Cottage
o. Shepherd's Cottage.
p. Close Cottage.

▨ Buildings existing in 1900 but since demolished.

A. The Forge.
B. Wheelwright's House & Shop.
C. Cottages.

APPROX. 200 FEET

TWENTIETH CENTURY
SNOWSHILL

Littleworth Cottages

High Beeches

Homepiece Cottages

Manor Cottages

Tower Close

Village Hall
(formerly the village school)

Hall's Piece

Post Office

Manor Barn

Snowshill Manor

Snowshill Arms

St. Barnabas Church

Old Barn

Little Hunrford

Green Close

Oat Hill Farm

Plan of village

43

Snowshill Remembered

The first half of the twentieth century was generally speaking a period of continuity in the appearance of Snowshill and in the way of life of its inhabitants although the seeds were sown for the far-reaching changes which were soon to occur.

At the turn of the century Snowshill was still, for the most part, divided into the two large estates, Snowshill Manor and Snowshill Farm, both with absentee landlords. The Manor, recently bought by John Wood, M.P., of Bury St. Edmunds, still comprised Manor Farm, farmed by Charles Lovesey, and Snowshill Hill, farmed by Kenyon Stow. Similarly Snowshill Farm belonged to Lord Redesdale and was farmed by George Hyatt. There were only two large houses, the Manor, which was in a very dilapidated state, and the much smaller Snowshill Farm House. Tower Close and Green Close were still clusters of cottages and had yet to be converted into the substantial houses they were later to become. Since the Second World War there has been a considerable amount of building and the old farm buildings have been converted into dwellings, but in the early years of the century there were in fact many more cottages than there are today, all of them old and stone-built and some of them in varying degrees of dilapidation. Next to Rose Cottage, which housed the successive school teachers and was then known as the School House, there was a stable belonging to Thomas Russell, the carter, who would take people to Evesham at six pence a time. By the stable were two cottages which adjoined Forge Cottage. These became dilapidated and were pulled down in about 1907. There were yet more cottages in a short terrace at right angles to Shepherd's Cottage just below the present Cotswold Cottage. All these appear on the six inch Ordnance Survey map of 1900 which was surveyed in 1882-1883.

Tower Close then consisted of three cottages. The cottage which was created by Don Smith in 1984 out of Tower Close garage was William Tom's dwelling before it became a garage and directly below it, down the steep bank and at right angles to the road, there were two further dwellings. Somewhat surprisingly there was quite a large cottage and a wheelwright's shop opposite the present Post Office, facing the road and backing on to the Church, in what is now part of the churchyard. It had a garden surrounded by wooden rails which also can be seen on the 1900 map and in an early photograph of the village. Although the cottage and wheelwright's shop were pulled down around 1907, George Diston remembers seeing Mr. Turner making wheels there. Green Close which belonged to the Manor used to be four

44

cottages in two groups of two separated by a path which passed just to the right of what is now the front door of the present house. There were also four cottages where there are now only two between the Snowshill Arms and Old Barn. One of these stood in what is now the entrance to the pub car park.

The row of cottages opposite the Manor is of particular age and interest. The tall malthouse had iron bars where the windows now are and housed a kiln for drying corn for malting. The garage on the right of the row was a farm outbuilding.

It was not until the late twenties that the roads in and around the village were given a surface of tarmac. Prior to this, they were just white tracks, rough at all times, dusty in summer and muddy in winter. Stone for Snowshill's roads came from the now disused quarry on the top of Oat Hill and it was dumped in heaps by the road. Men were paid by the heap to break the stone. This was a task usually undertaken by those who could not find other less arduous labour. It was not unknown for a villager to bicycle to the other side of Winchcombe in order to find work crushing stone. Once it had been crushed and left in a further heap, it was laid by council gangs and pressed down by a steam roller. The arrival of the steam roller was always a great excitement for the village children.

The roads into the village were gated. There was a gate beyond Green Close, another at the top of the bank by the turning to Brockhampton, one by what is now the Snowshill Manor Administrator's house, another on the road above it and one at the Tower Close cross-roads. These were removed around 1908. There were no fewer than four gates between the village and Snowshill Hill.

In the early 1900's, a farm labourer was earning about twelve shillings and six pence a week and, according to Smith and Ralph's "A History of Bristol and Gloucestershire", his wife would spend two and six pence on the week's shopping. There were two grocery shops in the village, one run by Mrs. Eliza Hodge and the other by David Smith in what is now Manor Farm Cottage. Early in the century, Herbert Keyte took over David Smith's business which moved to what is now The Old Shop. The business remained in the hands of the same family and on the same premises until after the Second World War when Mrs. Williams took over the Post Office. Happily, The Old Shop is still occupied by descendants of Mr. Keyte. The pub was in the hands of Edwin Beard who was the fourth member of his family to run it.

Snowshill Manor

In 1895, there was complicated litigation between the Sidebottom brothers and in the following year the whole of the Snowshill Manor estate and the several farms and cottages it contained, then totalling 1226 acres, was sold to John Wood, M.P.

On the 1st December, 1913, John Wood split the estate by selling Snowshill Hill and 406 acres to Kenyon Stow for three thousand pounds and, in June 1916, he offered the rest of the Manor for sale by auction through G. H. Bayley & Sons. Charles Lovesey was still living at the Manor House and was tenant of the remaining part of the estate but it had been arranged for him to give up possession at Michaelmas. Lovesey had long been regarded as Lord of the Manor but, as a tenant, it is most improbable that this was ever the case, particularly as the Lordship of the Manor was included in Lot 1 of the proposed sale. This lot included the Manor House, the Priest's House, then used as a dairy and granary, numerous outbuildings and 215 acres. There was also an option to purchase the cottages and malthouse on the other side of the road. The Manor House was described as "an attractive and substantial stone structure in original preservation but, like all such old world residences, offers many possibilities for judicious restoration".

Hill Barn Farm together with 246 acres was split into a separate Lot 2. Lot 3 was Tower Close which had been used as three tenements and was described as requiring restoration for occupation. This also included the garden and paddock and the plantation, on the opposite side of the road, two acres and thirty-three perches in all.

In Lot 4 was what described as an ivy clad cottage and the adjoining cottage. The first was the village shop which had now passed to Mr. Ernest Turner and was called "E. W. Turner, Grocer and Dealer in Tobacco". The other, then the School House and now Rose Cottage, was in the occupation of Mr. Walter Smith of the School Committee. Lot 5 comprised two small cottages and gardens which were situated between the Forge and Snowshill Farmhouse and which later became one house now called The Cottage. At the time of the auction in 1916, one of the two cottages was occupied by Mr. Henry Corbett and the other one was described as being "void".

In Lot 6 was the "Stone-built Tudor Residence" together with two cottages and gardens and a four acre field of old pasture known as Green Close. The house, then divided into two tenements, was believed to be older than the Manor House and its potential for development and being joined to one or both of the cottages was already anticipated.

The three (now two) cottages opposite the Church, on the Snowshill Arms side, were occupied by George Hands, Fred Chandler and Joseph Hands and comprised Lot 7. Lot 8 was the house opposite the entrance to the Manor.

It was a singularly unsuccessful auction because not only did the Manor fail to sell as a whole but only two of the eight lots found buyers. These were Tower Close which was sold to Mr. S. B. Russell and the two cottages in Lot 5.

A second auction was arranged two years later, also by G. H. Bayley & Sons, to take place on July 17th, 1918. Some changes had now occurred. The Manor and 214 acres comprised Lot 1. For some reason the eight acres of arable land on the South side of the road leading to Hill Barn Farm formed a separate Lot 2. The Manor by now appears to have acquired the four cottages opposite the Manor House and the malthouse, together with the land behind them. The cottages were occupied by Mrs. George Diston, Mrs. J. Spiers, R. Dyer and Mr. Newman and these, together with the house opposite the entrance to the Manor were offered as Lot 3. Green Close, Lot 4, by now had been "altered and improved at great expense and was in a perfect state of preservation". In the 1918 particulars of sale there are photographs of Green Close before and after alteration. The Turners' shop and the School House and the cottages opposite the Church were offered as before. The row of four cottages which include the present Post Office were offered for sale in 1918 as Lot 7. They were occupied by Albert Diston (known as Tommy), J. Folkes, T. Smith and Mrs. Nurdin, remembered for the wood pigeon she kept in a tea chest. Mr. Nurdin had been a shepherd which gave rise to the name Shepherd's Cottage.

Hill Barn Farm, occupied by Charles Lovesey, was Lot 8. Mr. Lovesey was paying an annual rent of one hundred and fifty pounds for the farm at the time of the auction.

The estate again failed to sell as a whole. A Yorkshireman, John Thomas Hull, bought the Manor Farm or Home Farm as it came to be known and Charles Lovesey bought Hill Barn Farm of which he had been tenant. Major R. H. Milvain was the purchaser of Green Close and it remains in his family to this day. Mrs. Milvain is particularly remembered for starting the Snowshill Women's Club in 1938 with Mrs. Ernest Turner and for the children's parties and coach trips to the pantomime which she used to arrange each year.

Charles Wade and Snowshill Manor

Charles Paget Wade of Yoxford, Suffolk, but with financial interests in St. Kitts in the West Indies, came across an advertisement in "Country Life" for Snowshill Manor in 1918. At the time he was serving as a sapper in France so it was not until February 1919 that he was able to visit Snowshill. Despite the grim weather and the general dilapidation of the property, Snowshill Manor immediately appealed to his imagination as a home for himself and his unique collection of craftsmanship. At this stage, the house had no garden, instead there was simply a rough farmyard overgrown with nettles, docks and thistles, and there were various farm buildings, sheds and a pig sty. The small house in the courtyard, known as the Priest's House, was the bake house and was in an equally deplorable state of repair and covered in ivy. The Priest's House is believed to have been so named because it is said to have been built on the site of a building used by priests from Winchcombe Abbey, while looking after the interests of the Abbot.

Having purchased the Manor and fourteen acres together with the two top cottages on the other side of the road for three thousand five hundred pounds, Charles Wade, who, as well as being an antiquary, was an architect, soon started to repair his new property. He employed some twenty-eight workmen from Gloucester who lived in the attic during the week. One of these refused to stay a second night because he said that the house was haunted. Wade later discovered that there was a tradition in the village about the ghost of one of the Benedictine Monks of Winchcombe Abbey. As it was so soon after the First World War and materials, particularly seasoned oak, were in short supply, the repairs took some three years to complete. During this time the garden was laid out and, until recently, it was believed that Wade was solely responsible for its design. This was a most reasonable assumption since it was a task which Wade was more than qualified to undertake, having won a prize in 1907 for the design of a garden somewhat similar to that of Snowshill Manor. Nevertheless, he commissioned M. H. Baillie Scott, an architect in Gray's Inn Square to design his garden and the result was very much in the spirit of the Arts and Crafts Movement, which was dear both to Wade and to Baillie Scott. The garden was laid out with terraces and walled enclosures, achieving a pleasant blend of the formal and the informal, and it incorporates such Arts and Crafts mannerisms as downpipes discharging into water barrels and dovecotes on the walls. To achieve all this, quantities of earth were carted from Mr. Hull's farm and also stone from the disused quarry on the hill. Charles Wade engaged William Hodge as his gardener, claiming that he liked his name and his mauve hat. Mr. Hodge was the only gardener and the garden was, if anything, more elaborate than it is today, so his must have been a hard job.

In his restoration of Snowshill Manor, Charles Wade removed discordant features which had arisen over the years and took infinite delight in the uneven surfaces and textures of the old walls, floors and ceilings. He was grateful for the window tax which had resulted in the blocking-off of some of the windows and so avoided cross-lighting which he disliked. In furnishing the house, Wade displayed his own idiosyncratic taste based on his ideas of design, colour and workmanship. He had begun collecting at the age of seven and Snowshill Manor offered him great scope to pursue this enthusiasm. It is thought unlikely that Wade ever lived, or contemplated living, in the Manor House but that he purely saw it as a setting for his collection and the models of his own creation. Instead, he chose to live in austere conditions in the small house in the courtyard.

Wade is remembered as a pleasant, if eccentric figure. Although he was seldom seen, he was always friendly to anyone he met. His appearance was strange with bobbed hair and breeches, stockings and buckled shoes. William Buchan in his biography of his father, John Buchan, recalls a visit to Mr. Wade that he made with his father and Virginia Woolf in July 1935. Having described Mr. Wade's appearance as giving a general impression of the eighteenth century, he went on to say that "his house inside was truly amazing, for Mr. Wade was a collector in the widest sense of the word. There were ancient looms and spinning wheels, and the tools of a dozen different crafts, sharing space with suits of Japanese armour. There was a fine collection of glass of all periods scattered about, and of course there was the crocodile. Wonders did not cease with the house. The outbuildings contained as astonishingly heterogeneous an assortment of objects from flowered silk waistcoats to astrolobes; and where a small stream ran below the house, a miniature harbour had been built with ships to scale and a complicated model railway system around". In 1932, John Betjeman, a frequent visitor to Snowshill, wrote about Wade's model Cornish village in the "Architectural Review". It was possibly the first model village in Britain.

Some five hundred people a year used to visit Snowshill Manor in Wade's lifetime and, from 1931, the garden was frequently open to the public in support of charities. He used to entertain generously and his guests included many writers and artists, such as F. L. Griggs, Edwin Lutyens, John Masefield and J. B. Priestley, who mentions his visit to Snowshill in 1933 in his "English Journey".

House guests used to sleep in the Manor House, often after an entertaining evening of unscripted play acting in the Hall. Wade, however, once his guests had retired to their candlelit bedrooms, would slip across the courtyard to his little cottage or in the summer to his garden bedroom by the pond, which he called "Jolly Roger".

In 1937, Queen Mary visited Snowshill Manor. She showed great interest in Charles Wade's collection but she is reported to have said that the finest thing in the house was Charles Wade.

Having given Snowshill Manor to the National Trust in 1951, Charles Wade emigrated to St. Kitts. He visited England in 1956 and was taken ill while staying in Broadway. He died shortly afterwards in Evesham Hospital and was buried in Snowshill churchyard.

Sydney B. Russell

In 1916, Sydney B. Russell, owner of the Lygon Arms in Broadway, bought Tower Close and converted the three cottages into one house. The pasture on which these cottages stood had long been known as Tower Close and so the tower which Russell incorporated into his conversion was obviously inspired by the old name rather than any justification for a new name. This was not Russell's first connection with the village as, before he completed the conversion of Tower Close, he had lived for some time at Green Close and was involved with its conversion from four cottages into a single substantial house. George Diston remembers the great influenza epidemic at the end of the Great War striking him and many in the village whilst he was living in Green Close with Mr. Russell.

S. B. Russell played an active role in the life of the village. Jack Hodge remembers that, to supplement their compulsory schooling, Mr. Russell gave extra reading lessons for eight to fourteen year olds on Sunday mornings, although presumably not on the one Sunday in the month when there was Holy Communion at 11 o'clock. On other Sundays, the only service was Evensong at 3 o'clock in the afternoon. Naturally, Mr. Russell's lessons were optional so sweets were handed round twice each session to encourage regular attendance. Mr. Russell used to read for about an hour. "Uncle Tom's Cabin" and "Puck of Pook's Hill" are particularly remembered and the children were expected to write an essay on the reading later in the week at school and prizes were awarded for the best essay. These lessons continued for two to three years until they came to an abrupt halt one Sunday. The book being read at the time was deemed to be boring and the children expressed their displeasure by writing deliberately poor essays. The following Sunday Mr. Russell demanded that the essays be rewritten, at which a voice at the back of the class refused, saying "I'm not going to". Mr. Russell was not prepared to tolerate such ill manners and the classes were never resumed.

During the nineteen-twenties, Charles Lovesey's health deteriorated and he sold Hill Barn Farm to S. B. Russell and moved to the village where his good friend, Miss Beard, nursed him in his final illness.

S. B. Russell had done much for the village but his sale of the Snowshill Forge and its contents to Henry Ford in 1929 was regretted by some. In the early years of the century the forge was still in use with the blacksmith, Charles Stanley, shoeing horses and doing all manner of repair work. George Diston remembers helping Mr. Stanley with the bellows. When Mr. Stanley became too old for the work, Fred Spragg came over from Laverton to help but gradually the business folded up and the forge fell into disrepair. The dilapidated forge caught the eye of

Henry Ford when he visited S. B. Russell and also Charles Wade in 1928. S. B. Russell bought the forge and the forge cottage from Miss Elizabeth Stanley in October 1929 and then sold the smithy to Henry Ford to dismantle and re-erect in Ford's outdoor museum in Dearborn, Michigan. A local contractor, Cox Howman, was employed to dismantle the building ready for shipment to the United States, together with its contents. Much of this work was done by the Diston brothers and George Diston remembers his father, George senior, numbering every stone to ensure that the smithy was re-erected correctly. He also remembers that his father had hoped to go to Dearborn to re-erect the building but in the end the task fell to a younger man.

S. B. Russell died in January 1938. He wanted to be buried in Campden so his coffin was taken from Tower Close on a farm waggon strewn with daffodils along the White Way to Campden Church, followed on foot by the funeral cortège. This was an old Cotswold tradition. It must have been a memorable sight and perhaps the last time that such would be seen along these lanes.

Mrs. S. B. Russell stayed on at Tower Close after the death of her husband in 1938 but, with the onset of war, her sons persuaded her to move back to Broadway. Tower Close was first let to friends and then sold to the Havillands in 1940 who, in turn, sold it to Hector Smith in 1947.

Snowshill Farm

In 1919, Lord Redesdale sold Batsford and his other lands in Gloucestershire. This included Snowshill Farm and the farm buildings on the opposite side of the road, now converted into the two houses, Little Hurnford and Old Barn. The long Hyatt tenancy had finally ended during the war with George Hyatt who is remembered with affection in spite of the fact that he used his riding crop to discourage children from collecting wood on Oat Hill. Walter Scott took over the farm for a few years. George Diston remembers Walter Scott's son joining in the Snowshill winter sport of a dozen or so children tobogganing down Oat Hill in a tin sheep trough. On one occasion, the lad nearly severed his thumb when the trough ran against a wall and he ran home to get it bandaged but all he received was a severe reprimand.

John Pennington Francis, a friend of John Hull and a fellow Yorkshireman, bought Snowshill Farm in 1920. Mr. Francis was, however, soon in financial difficulty. Failing to satisfy the Farmers' Land Purchase Company, to whom he had mortgaged the farm for six thousand pounds, the mortgagees foreclosed and Mr. Francis lost the farm. It was then let to L. G. Harris for £275 per annum. At this time Little Hurnford was a stable for eight horses and Nurk Meadows remembers that chaff for the horses used to be prepared by him in the adjacent barn, now Old Barn. He also remembers that in 1922 or 1923, he and his brother helped Jack Coppinger to build the staddle stone wall around the farmyard at the back of Old Barn which is now such a feature of the village. The staddle stones came from the old thatched oak beamed barn which used to stand at the North end of the row of cottages opposite the Manor. In 1923, Snowshill Farm was offered for sale at auction but failed to sell. However, in August 1925, 188 acres were sold to Mrs. Nancy Cawley of Snowshill Hill. Snowshill Farm was put on the market again in 1928 now with 363 acres, of which 350 were laid down to grass, but attracted no buyer. In June 1933, Snowshill Farm and 360 acres was at last successfully offered for sale by auction. It was presented in five lots with a reserve of two thousand pounds on Lot 1. This comprised the farm, the farmhouse and farm buildings and was then still let as a whole to L. G. Harris until the end of September. The farm was finally sold to Adrian Wells Beecham, of Stratford-on-Avon, for £3352.10s. He was the eldest son of Sir Thomas Beecham Bt. of the Beechams Powder family and of musical fame. Adrian Beecham kept his race horses at the farm and in 1940 he settled the property on Francis Channing Miles Wells by a vesting deed for life. Cottages were also included in the sale as separate lots. One described as Club Cottage fetched one hundred and ten pounds and Snowshill Farm Cottages sold for one hundred and twenty pounds.

On the 23rd October, 1942, Mr. Beecham and Mr. Wells, the trustees of the settlement, sold Snowshill Farm, which by then had 359 acres, to Arthur Gerald Porter, a farmer from Stevenage, for £5000. On the 2nd March, 1943, Porter sold 44.7 acres, including the buildings later to become Old Barn and Little Hurnford, to Robert Thomas Priestman. Eleven days later, Porter sold the farmhouse and 315 acres to Hector Smith of Offenham. In October 1964, Hector Smith sold the farmhouse and 15.8 acres to David Minet and by then the property had become known as Oat Hill Farm. Minet, in turn, sold it to Harry Fergusson-Wood in 1972. By 1980, much of Oat Hill Farm had been sold to Mr. and Mrs. Brian McDonald who have converted part of the farmhouse for use as holiday flats.

Snowshill Hill

Snowshill Hill had acquired a separate identity in 1913 when it was severed from the Manor and sold with 406 acres to Edward Kenyon Stow and his wife for three thousand pounds. They are described in the indenture as being "of Snowshill Hill" where they were previously tenants. According to Kelly's Directory, they had been there since at least 1906 but probably arrived shortly after 1897. Kenyon Stow is still remembered in the village with affection for the tea parties he used to give for the local children each summer.

In May 1916, Kenyon Stow sold to Mrs. Knox, of Spring Hill, 162 acres known as Campden Ash Ground, Rape Hill, Great Ground and Globe Hill for £2025 or twelve pounds and ten shillings an acre. On the 18th October, 1919, Kenyon Stow died and was buried at Snowshill but, prior to his death, he had agreed to sell Snowshill Hill to William Arthur Jukes. The sale went through on the 29th December of the same year. Jukes did not stay long and Snowshill Hill with 345 acres was put up for auction on the 21st July, 1923. The house was described as being Tudor "now modernised in excellent taste". A great attraction will have been that it had electricity, power as well as lighting, provided by a 20hp Ruston and Hornsby semi-diesel crude oil engine with compressed air starting. This provided lights for the residence, the bailiff's house and the principal farm buildings. The estate was described as being chiefly good grazing land with only two woods, one of 2 acres, 1 rood and 2 perches and Shippy Grove of 8 acres, 2 roods and 4 perches. Mrs. Nancy Burrell, a widow, purchased the estate for £9450 and the sale was concluded on the 11th December, 1924. On the following 14th February, appropriately perhaps, Nancy Burrell married James Donald Cawley who is remembered by Jack Hodge as an aristocratic gentleman but very much a countryman at heart, being more at home in the farmyard than in his 'going-to-London' clothes. He farmed mainly cattle and sheep but also some pigs and poultry.

John Bourne and Snowshill Hill

On the 1st June, 1932, John Bourne purchased Snowshill Hill, which then consisted of 532 acres, and so began a long period of continuity and growth in the history of the estate. For Mr. Bourne, who was born near Harrow in 1904 and educated at Rugby and Corpus Christi, Cambridge, this was the fulfillment of an undergraduate dream. From 1925 he was a director of Bourne and Hollingsworth, founded by his father and his uncle, and while working in London he also farmed at Watford until he moved to the Cotswolds. He brought four cows with him from Hertfordshire and with these he developed a herd of pedigree Ayrshires which, by 1953, was to become the most famous in the country. The Snowshill herd, which was the first herd of Ayrshires in England and Wales to become attested, twice won the Thousand Guineas Silcock Gold Cup for the best dairy herd in England and Wales. The herd also won the supreme championship in Scotland, which was a remarkable feat for an English herd. The Ayrshires were sold in 1962 and the farm is now largely arable, although two hundred thousand trees have also been planted in the last fifty years.

The farm has now grown to 740.736 acres with the acquisition of Smallthorns and Hornsleasow Farms.

Smallthorns had been Glebe land until July 1921, when the Reverend J. Wilfred Reynolds, rector of Stanton with Snowshill, with the approval of the Ecclesiastical Commission for England and the consent of the patron, Sir Philip Sidney Stott, sold the farm and 204 acres to John Meadows, who had been there for a number of years, for three thousand pounds. In 1939, John Bourne bought most of Smallthorns from John Meadows. He bought the farmhouse and 154 acres but excluded the cottage and lands on the Spring Hill side of the road. In 1978 Mr. Bourne sold Smallthorns farmhouse and the eighteen acres of Home Field to John and Mary Ellen Haig. Hornsleasow Farm with its 56 acres had for generations formed part of the neighbouring Wemyss Estate and is actually in the parish of Cutsdean. In 1942, however, it was purchased by John Bourne.

In 1982, John Bourne gave Hornsleasow farmhouse and four acres to his son, Christopher, who now runs the estate in partnership with his father.

Hector Smith

By 1936 there was a new farmer in the village, destined to become a principal landowner and a leading figure — Hector Smith. Hector Smith was born at the turn of the century in Offenham, the son of a local market gardener. He began as a fruit and vegetable wholesaler but his business expanded rapidly and he took over the Milcote Manor Farm near Stratford. In 1936, he bought Hill Barn Farm from S. B. Russell and was also tenant of Snowshill Farm which, as previously mentioned, he purchased from A. G. Porter in 1943. Hector Smith bought Tower Close in 1947 and lived there until his death. He was one of the pioneers of sprout growing in the Cotswolds and by the mid-nineteen fifties he was cropping one hundred and fifty acres although he gradually switched to corn. Mr. Smith is also especially remembered for his racehorses, of which he at one time owned twenty. He bred most of his horses himself and they also were trained at Snowshill. Mr. Smith died in 1979 and his Snowshill lands are now farmed by his son, Don Smith, and his son-in-law, Christopher Byrd.

Brockhampton

In 1916, the Phillipps estate, which comprised Middle Hill, Great Brockhampton and part of Little Brockhampton, was mortaged to Lloyds Bank and they exercised their right of sale by an auction on the 2nd March of that year. The estate was bought by Archibald Dennis Flower, who on the 9th December, 1918, sold Great Brockhampton Farm together with the Lordship of the Manor of Brockhampton to Captain C. T. Scott. The farmhouse was derelict and, around this time, was used by film makers to film a house on fire. In 1919, Captain Scott built two new farm cottages from the stone which had survived the blaze. They were built to a very high standard for farmworkers' cottages, each having a bathroom and parquet flooring, among other refinements. Captain Scott proudly put his initials and the date on the front. Mr. Alan Hunt farmed Great Brockhampton for seventeen years and he was succeeded by Mr. Mole. In 1947, Henry and Eila Harrison and their young family came to Great Brockhampton. They converted the two cottages into a farmhouse in 1963 and bought the farm from Captain Scott in 1966.

Manor Farm

Shortly before the Second World War, Mr. Hull sold Manor Farm to William Herbert Honor who built Field House on the right hand side of the road going towards Broadway. The farm buildings above the Manor, now converted and developed into a group of houses and known as Manor Barn, were used for cattle. These kept the village supplied with milk during the war. Mr. Honor also grew vegetables and alpine plants on a commercial scale. When he died, Mrs. Honor continued the alpine plant nursery with the asssistance of Frank Gunn and John Honour. Mrs. Honor is remembered as a generous benefactor of the village, especially where children were concerned, for whom she gave Christmas parties each year.

Local Government

The population of a parish has to include at least two hundred local government electors before it must have a Parish Council, and at least one hundred and fifty electors before the parish may, if it so desires, ask for such a council to be established. Snowshill, with approximately one hundred and forty on the Electoral Roll, has only a Parish Meeting. This is well attended and has an active committee elected annually but it only really has an advisory function and for most purposes is not a local authority. Since the reorganisation of local government on the 1st April 1974, under the Local Government Act 1972, Snowshill has come under

Tewkesbury District Council which is responsible for all local government matters except those such as highways, education and the fire service which are the responsibility of Gloucestershire County Council. Snowshill remains in the Winchcombe petty sessional division, that is within the jurisdiction of the Winchcombe magistrates, although they are in the course of being amalgamated into a North Cotswold bench which will be based on Stow-on-the-Wold. The headquarters of the sub-division of Gloucestershire Constabulary's 'A' Division into which Snowshill comes for policing purposes is also at Stow-on-the-Wold.

Village Life

The school took children from the age of about three to the leaving age of fourteen. Early in the century there were three classes and at one stage two teachers. Thereafter there was only one teacher and the number of classes was reduced to two, separated by a screen. The three to seven year olds were in one class and the seven to fourteen year olds in the other. At its peak, some fifty children attended the school. Children came from considerable distances including Snowshill Hill, Brockhampton, Stanway Ash, Kites Nest and Shenberrow.

There are no recollections of crime in the village at this time, juvenile or otherwise, but clearly there were plenty of high-spirited youngsters and youthful pranks. A favourite game was to use a bow to shoot the school mistress's cane into the ventilator in the school roof. The cane was invariably recovered and speedily used for its proper and painful purpose. 'Fox and Hounds' was commonly played at night and reels of cotton seem to have been essential equipment for young practical jokers. A much enjoyed prank was to attach a cotton thread, weighted with a button, to a window of the cottages opposite the Church. The thread was then pulled from across the street behind a gravestone so that the button tapped the window and the irate occupant was brought outside to chase the culprits. Even more enjoyable, was hiding on a haystack behind a low wall, now replaced by the staddle stone wall, and using a piece of cotton stretched across the road to knock off the hat of the school mistress's husband as he went to and from the pub. It is little wonder that various safe hiding places were sought. The most favoured seems to have been under a thatched oak beamed barn which stood on staddle stones at the North end of the cottages opposite the Manor. George Diston well remembers taking refuge there when one of Lovesey's bulls escaped and charged down the road.

After the 1914-18 War, a memorial to the dead was erected in the churchyard. The rector, Mr. Reynolds, commissioned Frederick Landseer Griggs, who did so much to restore Campden, to design it. At Reynold's suggestion, Griggs discussed the design with Charles Wade. Though in 1920 Wade was still a newcomer to the village, he would nevertheless have been interested in the war memorial both as a former soldier in the Great War and because of his profound interest in craftsmanship. No doubt S. B. Russell also approved of the choice of Griggs, who was a close friend of his son, the future Sir Gordon Russell. Indeed many years later, Sir Gordon, himself, was to carve a fine headstone for Griggs in the Catholic Church burial ground at Campden. The war memorial was made from stone from Stanton quarry donated by Sir Philip Stott. The stone was cut and erected by George Diston senior, his brother Albert and Jack Coppinger. The inscription reads simply, "In memory of those from this village who died for their country in 1914-18" and lists R. J. Aston, D. W. Diston, L. Diston, G. A. Hands and W. J. Hands.

It was also shortly after the First World War that an ex-army hut was erected behind Shepherd's Cottage on land owned by Mr. Russell. It began as a village hall for ex-servicemen and it was not until later that women were admitted. This hall was open six nights a week for snooker and, more often, billiards and was the centre of village life. Miss Beard, who by now had taken over the pub from her father, only allowed drinking on the premises. Darts and singing were not permitted and the local policeman quite frequently walked up from Stanton at night to make sure that there was no rowdiness in the village. After Mrs. Nurdin had gone, Shepherd's Cottage was used as a boiler room for the army hut village hall. The cottage had no staircase and consisted of just one room on the ground floor and one above which was reached by a ladder.

Mrs. Turner with the help of her husband, Ernest, who was severely crippled by arthritis, continued to run the village shop in the cottage now known as the Old Shop. Mrs. Edgworth remembers that her parents sold a wide range of goods, including boots, now, alas, factory made, but as necessary as ever. Charles Harrison used to bring the bread up in his pony and trap and this was laid out on a sheet in the Turners' shop. Before the Second World War, Mrs. Turner used to make ice-cream every day in a variety of flavours.

Before the days of the Post Office, there was a letter-box in the wall opposite the Manor gate. Harry Box, the Postman, used to walk from Broadway to Ford and back each day, blowing his whistle at the Manor gate and at Green Close to anounce his arrival. He brought stamps and scales to weigh the parcels and Charles Wade recalled seeing a parcel left by the roadside for the Postman to collect when he came by. The first Post Office was opened in 1928 in Bankside which was then two cottages and Mrs. Weatherall was the Postmistress.

In those years between the wars, Snowshill had little need of other shops as almost everything was delivered. The baker came nearly every day and no fewer than four butchers competed for custom, Collins and Robinson from Broadway and two from Blockley, of whom one alone, Balhatchet, still delivers. There were two general stores in Broadway, Midland Stores and Balls Stores. Dick Franklin was the outrider for Balls, coming up the hill on a bicycle to take orders. Having learnt the grocery trade, he set up on his own after the Second World War near the Swan Hotel and later his daughter, Barbara, married Ron Cook and the business became Franklin and Cook.

Young men used to wear suits more often than they do now and it was an annual event for Frank Lodge, the tailor, to come up from Bourton-on-the-Water to measure up those who could afford a new suit. These were usually the younger single men rather than those with family responsibilities. The new suits would be proudly worn for the first time at Easter.

Cricket was a major village pastime, so much so that there were two pitches, the boys' and the mens'. The former was in the field called Whitey Piece behind Maidenbright and the latter was on the lower and flatter part of the field out of which the National Trust car park has been created. By the early thirties, the men had become dissatisfied with the roughness of their field and the cowpats. Fortunately, Captain Walter Hannay came to the rescue and offered to create a proper pitch at Seven Wells on the Spring Hill estate. The wicket was laid by a firm in Cheltenham and the pitch could be mowed to the boundary. Cricket teas were prepared by Nancy Turner and the cakes were taken up in a pram and served at Seven Wells. Cricket, like so many other things stopped with the outbreak of war. There was not further cricket until the arrival of Hector Smith at Tower Close. He allowed the use of the field obliquely opposite the house. Jack Hodge was captain of the village team for six or seven years. He was succeeded by Henry Harrison. Cricket in the village ended in about 1965 when Mr. Smith needed the field for other purposes. For a while the team continued to play 'away' fixtures but gradually village cricket came to an end.

During the years between the wars, Snowshill Church boasted a choir of ten or twelve. It is remembered as a lively choir but at the same time "woe betide a child who so much as turned a hair of his head when he shouldn't do so". Services were well attended, especially by the children, and attendance might have been even higher if Evensong had not been at the awkward time of 3.00 pm.

In around 1927, the school, which had become a Church of England School, was closed for those over ten. The decision to do this was taken by the rector, Mr. Reynolds, and Major Milvain who believed it to be in the best interests of the children, a view not shared at the time by many in the village. In 1928, there were twenty-eight pupils but by 1932 the numbers had dwindled to eight and the school closed down. Responsibility for the school eventually passed to the Governors of the Gloucester Diocesan Council of Education in 1952 under a scheme relating to the Church of England Educational Foundations. Under this scheme, the Governors were authorised to sell the premises, provided that the price was approved by the Minister of Education. Accordingly, the Minister having given his approval on the 19th August, 1953, to a price of three hundred and fifty pounds, the school was sold on the 8th February, 1954, to four trustees who were to hold it on trust, under the terms of a trust deed of that date, for use as a village hall. The original trustees were Hector Smith of Tower Close, Charles Everett of Seven Wells Farm, Valentine Mary Honor of Field House and Robert Hannay of Spring Hill. As well as defining the purposes for which the hall may be used, the trust deed provides that it is to be administered by a management committee of not more than nine members.

Village Traditions

Snowshill is a village of traditions and possibly none more ancient than the Mummers. Until comparatively recently, Mummers' Plays with their local variations were an entirely oral tradition and therefore their origins are obscure but some believe that the plays are derived from Stone Age ceremonies when immortality was represented by singing and dancing. There were a number of versions of the Mummers' Play in the Cotswolds. The version last performed in Snowshill, which came from Blockley, is one of the few to have survived into the second half of the twentieth century and to have been written down. The full script is set out in Appendix VII. It was William Hodge and George Diston who revived the tradition after the First World War and the play continued to be performed each Christmas Week until the outbreak of the Second World War. It has been revived since and was last performed in the Great Hall of the Manor House in 1970. After the First World War, most of the original cast of eight were ex-servicemen and they performed in pubs, large houses and cottages, where, by arrangement, groups of spectators had gathered. They would go to Broadway, Stanton, Stanway and Buckland or anywhere within cycling range although the journey home was more often than not on foot, the cast being in no fit state to ride their bicycles. The play lasted about twenty minutes and the cast included Father Christmas, who introduced the show, King George who offered to fight all comers, Bold Slasher who fought and killed King George, the Doctor, assisted by Finney who ran in and out with medical instruments and Beelzebub, who terrified the children and whose main task seems to have been to take a collection in a frying pan, known as a dripping pan. This was said to be a symbol of the one used to baste lost souls. The limited story involved the doctor extracting a huge tooth from the dead King George whereupon he revived. All this was accompanied by the mimed "music" of Fiddler Wit.

The production of the Mummers' play was most carefully prepared and William Hodge for one, took the study of his few lines with the utmost seriousness "as though it were Shakespeare".

Another landmark in the Snowshill calendar each year was St. Barnabas Day on the 11th June, the Patronal Festival. It used to start with a tea party for the children in the school arranged by Mrs. Ernest Turner. This was followed by tea for the adults at 5.0 pm. Then there was a long procession round the green to the Church, headed by a neighbouring Brass Band playing "Onward Christian Soldiers". A service was held in the Church and this was followed by dancing in the evening. Miss Spiers, the infants' teacher played the violin and the "Snowshill Swing" or "Snowshill Swedish" was danced. This was danced in groups of six and the dancers would sing:-

Charlie had a fiddle worth a piece of gold
Once it was a new one, now it's very old.

Like the Mummers, this tradition ceased with the outbreak of the Second World War.

The fair used to come to Snowshill once a year on the Saturday after Whitsunday and this occasion was known as the Snowshill Wake. Snowshill Wake always followed fairs held in both Ford and Broadway the previous week and swings, roundabouts and other fairground equipment were hauled into Snowshill from both places to create as large a fair as possible. It must have been a tremendous sight as the swings and roundabouts filled the road, the village green and the close now occupied by the house known as Hall's Piece. The close also housed a large marquee from which Mr. Beard sold beer as well as selling it in the pub. People crowded into Snowshill from miles around, drawn not only by the entertainment but also by the home-made wine for which the village was locally famed. It was said the crowds were such that you could "walk round the churchyard on people's heads". Snowshill Wake was in its heyday in the years before the First World War. In the early twenties, a Mr. Bannerman, known as "Cheap-Jack", used to come up from Burford with a horse-drawn covered wagon filled with bric-a-brac in which he did a lively trade. Later, the Wake moved to a new site near the present National Trust car park but, to the sorrow of the local children, it came to and end in the early thirties.

Guy Fawkes Day too was always celebrated with an enormous bonfire on the village green.

Snowshill Today

The first council houses to be built in Snowshill, Church View and Vale View, were erected by Winchcombe Rural District Council on land which was sold to them by John Wood, M.P., on 24th October, 1914, and on which there had previously been two dilapidated cottages between The Old Forge and Rose Cottage. These original council houses came into private ownership in the nineteen thirties. The main twentieth century development of Snowshill, however, began around 1939-40 when a second set of council houses, a block of four, was built. These were needed to rehouse the occupants of the row of cottages which ran down the bank from the top road and which had fallen into disrepair. The derelict cottages were finally demolished after the war. More council houses followed which rehoused the inhabitants of cottages which absentee landlords had allowed to deteriorate. Captain Walter Hannay, of Spring Hill, gave two hundred pounds in order that the new council houses could be built of stone and so blend happily into the environment. Captain Hannay also bought Springhill Cottages around 1937. These were modernised with extensions at the back and new dormer windows.

In 1958, the year in which the Reverend Michael Bland became rector of Stanton cum Snowshill in a newly united benefice with Buckland, a small alteration was made to the external appearance of the Church. When St. Barnabas was built in 1864, it had been intended, as previously mentioned, that it should have a spire but as the funds had not been forthcoming, a temporary slate roof had been placed on top of the tower. This was not only ugly but it had also fallen into disrepair and so it was decided to remove it altogether, leaving just the tower with a flat roof. The work was carried out by Alfred Groves Limited of Milton-under-Wychwood and the architects were Stretton, Davis and Yates. The cost was £519 14s. 6d. which compares interestingly with the £1700 it cost to build the entire Church less than a century before. The money for this small but neccesary alteration was raised by a fête organised by Robert Hannay.

It was in the nineteen-fifties that life in Snowshill underwent radical changes, partly for the better and partly, some might say, for the worse. Of the greatest benefit, undoubtedly, was the connection of running water and electricity during that decade which must have made life for all immeasurably less arduous and more comfortable.

The National Trust

An event which was to make a great impact on the life of the village was the gift in 1951 of Snowshill Manor by Charles Wade to the National Trust. It was opened to the public on the 3rd May 1952 by Professor Richardson, the eminent architect and friend of Charles Wade, who had written a long article about the Manor in the 1st October 1927 issue of "Country Life". Snowshill was now firmly on the tourist map and would never be quite the same again, at least during the summer months, when the village is sometimes filled to capacity with cars and coaches. One suspects that Charles Wade who lived in a world of his own, never anticipated that his gift to the National Trust of his home and his unique collection would attract so many to the village. It should however be said that even if he had not made his gift, such an idyllicly beautiful village as Snowshill, could not, in this age of the motor car, expect to escape the attentions of city-dwellers in search of the countryside. Those of us who are privileged to enjoy this beauty all the year round must expect to share it with others at least during the summer months.

The Snowshill Arms

Other factors, however, have also wrought change in the life of Snowshill. The Snowshill Arms, under the management of Hans Schad, attracts customers from far and wide, but this is a recent phenomenon, or rather a revival. Around the turn of the century, the Snowshill Arms was considerably enlarged with the addition of the South wing. This was used for private functions, such as shooting parties. In 1911, Edwin Beard, the publican, died and his daughter, Blanche Ada Beard, took over and continued to run it until her retirement, at the age of ninety-two, in 1968. In those days, the entrance to the pub was through a door, now blocked up, in the centre of the front of the building. Inside, a door to the left led to a private sitting room, seldom used, and on the right was the pub which contained no bar but just a high backed settle and two small chairs by the fire side. The room at the back, which is now the kitchen, was Miss Beard's living room, into which friends and sometimes customers' children were invited. There were two sets of stone steps. One set led from behind the present bar down to her private kitchen. The other set were quite literally worn to the shape of her feet and led down to the beer cellar, beneath the present kitchen. It is recalled that Miss Beard was a large woman and that, although aflicted with a chest complaint, she had amazingly strong wrists and could carry five pints up from the cellar in one hand. This was a very useful strength in the absence of a bar as each order had to be brought up from below. No spirits were sold, only Donnington's beer and cider.

By 1955, Miss Beard's health was deteriorating and so too was the pub and she was in danger of losing her licence, so Donnington Brewery bought the premises from Miss Beard but allowed her to remain there as a tenant at a rent of four shillings a year and to run the pub as she wished. The condition of the pub continued to deteriorate until 1968 when, with reluctance and, in a sense, to the regret of her friends who remember her with fondness, Miss Beard finally retired. There was pressure to close the pub down altogether. Donnington Brewery in fact closed it for a year during which they thoroughly renovated it. On the 20th December, 1969, it was reopened by Sir Gerald Nabarro, M.P., and it was managed by Alistair Biles until his retirement in 1979 when it was taken over by Hans Schad. September 1981 saw the opening by Bob Hodge of the skittle alley, which added another facet to Snowshill life.

In Conclusion

Inevitably the twentieth century, more than any other, has been a time when families have drifted apart and away from their roots in search of work. This has of course been true of Snowshill but happily there remains a core of centuries old Snowshill families. Of course property changes hands, new houses are built or extended and newcomers arrive. Proverbially newcomers take twenty-five years to be accepted but in reality there is a great wealth of kindness which finds a united expression each summer when the village rallies in support of the fête, which is an invariably happy and successful occasion. The fête raises funds for the maintenance of the Village Hall, the former school building, now used for a variety of purposes including the Snowshill Womens' Club, various village gatherings and the childrens' Christmas party, which for many years was organised by Mrs. Williams who has always done so much for the children of the village.

Sadly the old traditions of the Mummers, St. Barnabas Day, cricket, the Snowshill Wake and Bonfire Night which punctuated each year, have probably gone for ever. In this age of the motor car, television and more comfortable homes, village people tend to look elsewhere for their pleasure. However, Blockley Brass Band and various troupes of Morris Dancers perform regularly on the village green, giving pleasure to locals and visitors alike.

In spite of all the changes of the centuries and particularly of the last thirty to forty years, there is a thread of continuity which links our Bronze Age ancestors with ourselves. The fields around Snowshill have since the days of the earliest settlers reverberated with the sound of sheep and they continue to do so. It is to be hoped that they always will.

Appendix I

**A description of the Bronze Age barrow excavated by
William Greenwell M.A., D.C.L., F.R.S., F.S.A., at
Snowshill in 1891 and of the artefacts he found.**[1]

Greenwell's barrow was sixty-six feet in diameter and although it had
been reduced by ploughing it was still, before the excavation, five and
half feet high. At the centre and partly sunk below the level of the
surface was a cist made from four slabs of oolite set on edge, covered by a
fifth slab. It was four feet long, three feet wide and two and a half feet
deep and contained the skeleton of a man, presumed to be a warrior,
with two bronze daggers, a crutch-headed bronze pin and a perforated
axe-hammer of stone. One of the daggers, which is 9½ inches long and
2⅜ inches wide where the handle joins the blade, is of a particularly
unusual form and obviously a superbly made and powerful weapon.
The other dagger is slightly smaller, more usual in design and generally
less impressive. Both, however, are regarded as archaeological
prototypes of what is called the Cameron-Snowshill dagger series. The
pin, similar to others found in Wiltshire, is 6⅝ inches long with a head
about ⅝ of an inch wide. Like the larger dagger, the stone axe-hammer
is most beautifully made and highly polished. It is 6½ inches long and 2½
inches wide at the cutting edge. Dr. S. P. Needham, research assistant in
the Department of Prehistoric and Romano-British Antiquities of the
British Museum, confirmed in 1985 that these four objects are of British
manufacture although the pin has generalised parallels in Europe and
may be of continental inspiration. Dr. Needham dates the objects firmly
within the second stage of the so-called "Wessex Culture" at the end of
the Early Bronze Age circa 1600-1400 BC.

The larger dagger and the axe-head display a very high standard of
workmanship and reflect the fact that the inhabitants of the Snowshill
area in the Early Bronze Age were far from primitive. By this time such
people were living in wooden houses in permanent settlements and
farming techniques had become quite advanced, although uplands were
preferred to lowlands as the soil is light and easier to cultivate. There
were already complex trading systems in operation both within the
length and breadth of England and Wales and also with the Continent.
Indeed it is known that even in the earlier Neolithic age, "axe factories"
in various parts of the country were producing tools for distribution
over a wide area via the ancient trackways. The rich contents of the
Snowshill barrow, including an artefact of possible continental

inspiration, clearly suggest that these early settlers participated in the fairly advanced culture of Wessex to the South.

1.   Rev. William Greenwell, M.A., D.C.L., F.R.S., F.S.A., Recent Researches in Barrows in Yorkshire, Wiltshire, Berkshire etc. *Archaeolgia*, 1890 pp.70-72.

Appendix II

Shenberrow Camp[1]

Shenberrow Camp was partially excavated in July 1935 by students from the Universities of Cambridge and London. The finds resulting from this excavation are consistent with intensive occupation of the site by Iron Age A farming communities. There were prolific remains of sheep, together with those of horses, oxen and dogs and the flora and fauna were similar to those found today. There were two entrances to the camp, one by a trackway from the South-West and the other from the North-East, probably by the route which links Shenberrow Farm with Snowshill. The Western edge follows the line of the escarpment although much of this outer rampart has been destroyed. However it is clear that there were once formidable bivallate defences enclosing an area of two and a half acres. The inner rampart has been protected by trees and the outer ditch and rampart can clearly be seen where the entrance from the Snowshill direction cuts through them at the North-East. Further to the East, the ditch and rampart have been reduced by ploughing and partly destroyed by the Shenberrow farm buildings, although, fortunately, the interior of the camp did not appear to have been ploughed.

In the North-Western rampart nineteen sherds or fragments of shelly Iron Age A pottery with a buff brown outer surface have been found. Considerable evidence of occupation has been found at the junction of the North-West and South-West stretches of the rampart and this is thought to have been the site of a rectangular hut. This was probably a lean-to construction with the roof leaning on the angle of the ramparts but held up at the free corner by a single post. There was wood ash in what appears to have been a fire place. Numerous Iron Age sherds have been found nearby, together with needles, whetstones, a stone spindle whorl, stone rubber, pebbles foreign to the area, fragments of an iron ring, possibly part of a brooch, a bronze bracelet with a ring and dot decoration and a broken bronze finger ring. Such a diverse collection of practical and decorative objects indicates a fairly advanced and settled way of life.

Above the level of the Iron Age finds were those from the Romano-British settlement of the second century A.D. These included sherds of pottery, an iron knife, two iron nails, a chip of iridescent glass and pieces of flint together with a large quantity of sheep bones. The South-West rampart had an inner face of dry stone walling three feet high.

1. C. I. Fell, Shenberrow Hill Camp, *T.B.G.A.S.* Vol. 80, 1961, pp.16-41

Appendix III

"Men and Armour for Gloucestershire in 1608"

Explanation of the abbreviations used in the extract from the above:

The figure 1 indicates an age of about twenty.

The figure 2 indicates an age of about forty.

The figure 3 indicates an age of between fifty and sixty.

The letter "p" shows that the man was "of the tallest stature" and tall enough to be a pikeman.

The letter "m" shows that the man was of medium height, sufficiently tall to be a musketeer.

The letters "ca" show that the man was of shorter stature. He was not tall enough to be a musketeer but was nevertheless tall enough to be armed with a caliver (a light kind of harquebus, or portable fire-arm, which could be fired without a rest or support).

The letters "py" show that the man was "of the meanest stature" and only fit to be a pioneer "or of little other use".

The letters "tr" show that the man was a trained soldier at the time the list was compiled.

The letters "sub" indicate that the man was a "subsidy man" at the time, as opposed to a trained soldier.

Appendix IV

Land comprising Snowshill Manor
at the time of the Indenture of 7th June 1638

At the time of the indenture of June 7th, 1638, Snowshill Manor which was described in the deed as "the Manor House Farm or Grainage of Snowshill", comprised the following land. Enclosed ground called The Penny (3 acres), closes called Home Close (6 acres), Lord's Close (10 acres), Phillip's Close (5 acres), Stacking Close (6 acres), Ram Close (4 acres), Lower Meadow (16 acres), Upper Meadow (8 acres), Bryer Furlong (8 acres), Sheep Hay (60 acres) and a further Sheep Hay (5 acres). It also included parcels of land in common fields of Snowshill called Walle Furlong (30 acres), Deane Furlong (30 acres), Whiteway Piece (15 acres), Home Furlong (15 acres), Broad Piece (9 acres), Stone Piece (4 acres), Curnock Piece (4 acres), and New Close (4 acres). Further included was a sheep walk for six hundred sheep called the Lord's Sheepwalk or Abbot's Hogg Flock lying next to Seven Wells, a sheepwalk called How's Meadow or, again, the Lord's Sheepwalk (also for six hundred sheep) lying next to Hornsleasow, a sheepwalk (400 sheep) in the slate quarries, sheepwalk for one year, and in the next year in the sheepwalk down the middle of the hill. Also sheepwalks called Rowdon and Threrrall Breach and parcels of land called Horse Close (2 acres) and Clay Piece (5 acres); five acres of land in Deane Furlong, common pasture for two beasts and twenty sheep on the wastelands of Snowshill, a cottage and land in Catchill and eight acres of land-shooting into Royden Furlong in Snowshill.

Appendix V

The Schedule to the Indenture dated 13th August, 1860

The Schedule referred to by the before written Indenture

No. on Plan			a.	r.	p.
1	Home Meadow including Plantation road and pits	Arable		39	0
1a	Shepherds house yards and garden				1
2	Spring Ground exclusive of public road	Arable		41	1
3	Campden Ash ground	"		34	3
4	Rape Hill with drift and sheep pens	"		54	3
6	Rickyard Field exclusive of public road but including all others	Arable	45	3	25
7	Cottage and garden by Rickyard		0	0	17
8	Rickyard			3	20
9	Snowshill farm yards and buildings			3	29
10	The Farm house and garden			1	36
11	Sheep Hay Pool Ground including Roadway and pond	Pasture	13	1	32
12	Rickyard meadow	"	10	2	25
13	Ox Sheppy	Arable	18	1	27
14	The Park	Pasture	5	0	9
15	The Little ditto	"		3	21
16	Sheppy	Arable	19	3	22
17	Ditto Grove	Wood	5	0	3
18	Grove Ground	Arable	41	2	34
19	Great Ground exclusive of public road	"	53	2	37
20	Globe Hill	"	27	3	22
21	Barn & yard			1	22
46	Little Meadow	Meadow	9	1	2
45	Hitching Coppice		2	3	22
47	Town Meadow		15	0	5
48	Reedy Coppice	Wood	3	1	20
49	Widderksley	Meadow	17	1	7
		A	463	3	8

In the occupation of Mr. John Marshall at the rental of £225 per annum

Snowshill or the Manor Farm

No.	Name	Type			
22	Spring Hill Ground	Arable	49	1	14
23	Seven Wells ditto exclusive of public road	„	41	2	10
24	Great Hill ditto	„	58	1	12
25	Grove Piece	„	38	2	39
26	Sheep Hay Grove	Wood	4	1	3
27	ditto	„	2	2	15
28	Sheep Hay pasture including Oxhouse and yard	Pasture	50	2	13
29	Sheep Hay lane exclusive of public road	„		1	4
30	Further Slate Pits	Arable	20	2	5
„	Waste Hills and road in ditto	Pasture	11	2	7
37	Hither Slate Pits	Arable	25	0	30
36	Claypit Ground exclusive of public road	Arable	41	1	3
31	The several	„	38	2	3
32	The Rubbing Stack exclusive of public road	„	37	2	27
33	Barn Hill or picked piece	„	41	1	12
34	Honey Hill exclusive of public roads	„	45	2	36
	Wastes in ditto	Grass	2	1	3
35	Hill Barn sheds and yard			3	28
38	Barn Ground exclusive of public roads	Arable	36	1	19
39	Home Ground ditto and quarries		43	2	15
39a	Town Quarries and wastes in ditto	Grass	4	1	16
40	Broadway Wood ground	Arable	43	0	15
40a	Town Quarry etc. in ditto	Grass			37
41	Upper Hitching exclusive of public road	Arable	38	1	21
42	Hitching Plantation	Wood	1	0	15
43	ditto	do	1	1	39
44	Lower Hitching exclusive of public bridle way	Arable	11	0	29
50	Snows Meadow	Meadow	13	2	30
51	Coppice	Wood		2	34
52	Lower Meadow with a Shed	Pasture	13	2	37
53	Upper of Lower ditto	do	7	2	1
54	Lane to Meadows			1	14
55	Home Close	Pasture	10	3	36
56	Lords Close	do	8	1	7
56a	Coppice	Wood		1	11
57	Green Close	Meadow	4	0	38
58	Garden Coppice	Wood		1	24

No.	Description	Type			
59	Garden	Garden		1	33
60	Orchard	Pasture	1	1	4
61	Yard				8
62	House yards and buildings		1	1	34
63	Rickyard			1	20
93	Garden				21
91	Tower Close	Pasture	1	2	25
90	Three tenements and gardens				38
89	Garden				14
92	Cottage and garden				16
85	Garden plots			1	9
78	Cottage and garden				15
79	do do				15
80	Shed and ditto				14
64	do do				20
68	Cottage				1
65	Garden				16
69	Cottage and Garden				7
67	Garden and Hovel				16
71	Cottage				27
		A	759	2	35

In the occupation of Miss   and Miss   Marshall as yearly tenants at a rental of £550 per annum.

Cottages etc. in the Village of Snowshill

		Tenant			
70	Cottage and garden	R. Woodward			
	Coal shed	Held by Parish			13
	Granary	Late Marshall			
66	Cottage and garden	R. Harris			6
72	A parcel of garden ground	Thomas Hyatt			4
		paying quit rent of 1/-			
73	Two cottages and gardens	J. Cobbet & R. Stanley			17
		(probably Corbett)			
81	Cottage and garden	C. Turner			19
82	do do	I. Turner			15
83	do and shop	I. Bustin			4
84	A Shed and Waste	Held at a quit rent			1
		of 2/6			
86	House and garden	Miss Smith			15
87	Plantation				33
88	The Pound				3
77	Three Cottages	W. Hands, I. Stanley			15
		& I. Harris			
75	Garden	I. Stanley			17
76	do and Hovel	W. Hands			6
74	do	I. Harris			4
			A	1 0	12

All let to yearly tenants at Rentals amounting together to £36-4-0 per annum.

5	Plantation and pond	2 0 31

In the occupation of General Lygon at the rental of £3 per annum.

Appendix VI

Rectors of Stanton with Snowshill

1269?	John de Tueing
1269	Robert de Northleach
1298	Henry de Dydebrook
1311	William Boveton
1339	John de la Hulle
1341	Stephen de Ganeburgh exchanged with John atte Grove
1362?	Thomas Proud
1433	Henry Halyng exchanged with William Woky
1445	William Danyellis
1458	Richard Hawkes
1498	Maurice Westbury
1545	Kenelm Deane
1571	Robert Clutterbrucke
1591	Lawrence Banckes
1623	Henry Izod
1650	Thomas Vyner
1668	Henry Kirkham R.A.
1700	Lionel Kirkham R.A.
1736	Thomas Woods M.A.
1759	Robert Kirkham Ll.B.
1765	William Barnes M.A.
1766	Hudson Boyce
1771	Reginald Wynniatt Sr. M.A.
1819	Reginald Wynniatt Jr. M.A.
1838	William Henry Bloxome
1877	Morris Burland Harris Burland M.A.
1911	Thomas Wilfred Reynolds M.A.
1938	Eric William Bradley Cordingly A.K.C.
1941	John Emmanuel Scrope-Howe A.K.C.
1945	Robert Milburn Crowe M.A., B.D.
1948	Benefice vacant
1958	Michael Bland M.A.

Appendix VII

Text of the Mummers Play
as last performed at Snowshill

Characters

Father Christmas	
King George)	
Bold Slasher)	Dressed as soldiers
Doctor	Dressed in top hat and long-tailed coat
John Vinney	Dressed as a groom
Beelzebub	Dressed in tattered coat and long beard: looks rough: carries club and frying pan
Fiddler Wit	Like a man in the street with a fiddle: black face: some thin strips of rag on his coat

All have their faces painted

— — — — — —

Father Christmas knocks at the door, is let in carrying a broom. He begins sweeping the room and says:
> In comes I, old Father Christmas, Christmas or not,
> I hope old Father Christmas will never be forgot;
> Roast beef, plum pudding and mince pies,
> Never did old Father Christmas like these better than I.
> A room, a room, a gallant room and give us room to reign,
> For we to show our bold activities this merry Christmas time.
> And if you don't believe all I say, walk in,
> King George, and clear the way!
> (sweeps floor)

King George:
> In comes I, King George, King George, this noble knight,
> Who shed his blood for Briton's bright;
> What makes me carry this blood weapon
> Is because I have fought many a hard battle at home and abroad;
> And if any man here can conquer me
> A French Captain Collier he shall be.

Father Christmas:
> Walk in, Bold Slasher.

Bold Slasher:
> Bold Slasher, Bold Slasher, Bold
> Slasher is my name;
> I come to fight this champion,
> King George is called his name;
> I'll cut him, I'll hack him,
> I'll cut him as small as flise
> And send him to Jamaica
> To make mince pies.

King George:
> Mince pies I do not like but a battle with you I will fight.
> (They go into battle and King George is slain)

Father Christmas:
> Oh, is there a doctor to be found all ready near at hand?
> Who'll cure this deep and deadly wound and make this dead
> man stand?

Doctor (walks in):
Oh, yes, there is a doctor to be found all ready at hand.
Who will cure that deep and deadly wound and make that dead
man stand.
Father Christmas:
What canst thee cure?
Doctor:
Oh, I can cure imples, pimples, simples, itch, the stitch,
the palsy and the gout;
Pain within and pains without;
And if the old man is in him I can fetch him out.
Father Christmas:
What is thy fee then, Doctor?
Doctor:
Five pounds my fee;
Ten pounds I ask before I set that gallant free.
Father Christmas:
Work thy will then, Doctor.
Doctor:
Where does this very bad pain lie?
Father Christmas:
In his upper lower jaw.
Doctor:
How long has he suffered this very bad pain?
Father Christmas:
A fortnight or three weeks before it came.
Doctor:
Why did you not send to me before it came?
Father Christmas:
'Cos I didn't know where thee lived.
Doctor:
I lives here and nowhere else long;
I bin up in the Black Country 'mongst the gentiles,
    Killing all and curing none;
Italy, Sicily, France and Spain, now I return to old
    England again.
(Calls his assistant, John Vinney)
Jack Vinney!
(J. Vinney enters, carrying a haversack with a pill box and a
bottle of medicine, pair of pliers and spectacles in it)
J. Vinney:
My name is not Jack Vinney.
Doctor:
What is thy name?

J. Vinney:
My name is Mr. John Vinney, a man of great strength.
Do as much as thee or any other man;
Chop a good magpie's yud off and throw him in the ditch
And fetch him out in three months' time
As good a magpie as ever you did see.
Walk up and down the street in a purr of pattens.
Doctor:
That's all very fine, John, what other diseases?
J. Vinney:
Just as your medicine pleases.
Doctor:
Fetch me my spectacles, Jack Vinney.
J. Vinney:
Shant, fetch 'em theeself then.
Doctor:
What's that?
(J. Vinney goes running to fetch them out of his haversack)

76

J. Vinney:
Just a 'coming, Sir.
(Doctor puts on spectacles and examines the man)
Doctor:
Ah, ah, ladies and gentlemen; this man is suffering from the toothache very bad indeed.
Fetch my pliers, Jack Vinney.
J. Vinney:
Fetch 'em theeself, then.
Doctor:
What's that?
J. Vinney:
Just a 'coming, sir.
(Runs to get them out of the haversack)
Doctor:
Now, my men, as strong as elephants,
See if you can ease this poor man for me.
(Doctor on bended knees, with pliers and horse's tooth hidden in his hands; J. Vinney and Bold Slasher on knees pull at the
doctor's waist to draw out the tooth. Father Christmas leans on
his broom and watches)
Father Christmas:
Look, look, ladies and gentlemen; more like a horse's,
elephant's or a camel's tooth than a Christian's. Why,
it would carry a quarter of beans across the rough, rocky
road and never drop one.
Doctor:
Fetch my pills, Jack.
J. Vinney:
Fetch 'em theeself then.
Doctor:
What's that?
J. Vinney:
Just a 'coming, sir.
(Runs to get them)
Doctor:
Ladies and gentlemen, these are the most wonderful pills
in the world. I cured Jack Giggins' wife with one of
these yere small pills; she done no more than she done
no less and after that she died it took nine blind men
to lower her down through the roof of the house in case
she should fall and break her neck.
(Doctor then gives King George a pill)
Doctor:
Fetch the medicine.
J. Vinney:
Shant, fetch it theeself.
Doctor:
What's that?
J. Vinney:
Just a' coming, sir.
(Runs to get it)
Doctor:
Ladies and gentlemen, this is Garland's blood mixture; it
will fetch a man back to life in a few seconds; apply a
spot to his brow and a spot to his heart.
Arise, King George and fight thy part.
(King George jumps up)

Beelzebub (comes in in a threatening attitude, club on shoulder and
frying pan in hand):
    In come I, Beelzebub,
    On my shoulder I carry my club;
    In my hand the dripping pan;
    Don't you think I'm a jolly old man?
    Now then you yellow asses and black
      faces, can't you agree?
    Last Christmas Eve I turned the spit;
    I burnt my finger and felt it hit;
    A spark flew over the table
    And the pot lid beat the ladle;
    King Jack stood up like a noble man,
    Said he'd fight the dripping pan;
    The dripping pan with his long tail
    Swears he'll take you all to jail.
Fidler Wit:
    In comes I, Fidler Wit,
    With my great yud and little wit;
    Me yud so big, me wit so small,
    I brought my fiddle to please you all.
    What tune, ladies and gentlemen?
    Oh, the old favourite(s) —
    Ran Tan, the tinder box;
    Jack up the orchard;
    Cat in the fiddle bag.
All sing "Darkies lead a happy life" while the collection is taken in the frying pan.

Notes

Prehistory to Domesday

1. Rev. William Greenwell, M.A., D.C.L., F.R.S., F.S.A., Recent Researches in Barrows in Yorkshire, Wiltshire, Berkshire etc., Archaeologia, 1890, pp.70-72.
2. Christopher Taylor, Roads and Tracks of Britain, J. M. Dent & Sons, 1979, p.184.
3. G. R. Crosher, Along the Cotswold Ways, Cassell, 1976, p.19 (Pan Edition).
4. Helen O'Neil, Transactions of the Bristol and Gloucestershire Archaeological Society (T.B.G.A.S.), Vol. 86, 1967, p.30.
5. G. R. Crosher, Along the Cotswold Ways, pp.66-67.
6. C. I. Fell, Shenberrow Hill Camp, T.B.G.A.S., Vol. 80, 1961, pp.16-41.
7. H. P. R. Finberg, The Gloucestershire Landscape, Hodder & Stoughton, 1975, p.17.
8. Josceline Finberg, The Cotswolds, Eyre Methuen, 1977, p.68.
9. Anglo-Saxon Chronicle, translated by Anne Savage, Papermac, 1982, p.41.
10. Brian Smith and Elizabeth Ralph, A History of Bristol and Gloucestershire, Phillimore, 1972-82, pp.22-25.
11. Anglo-Saxon Chronicle, p.51.
12. Josceline Finberg, The Cotswolds, p.73.

Snowshill under the Abbey of Winchcombe

1. Domesday Book — Gloucestershire, translated by John S. Moore, Phillimore, 1982, p.165.
2. Landboc sive Registrum Monasterii de Winchelcumba, ed. D. Royce, 1903, Vol. I, pp.71-72.
3. Bishop Reynolds Register, 1308-1313, Worcestershire Record Office.
4. Landboc, Vol. I, p.143, Vol. II p.217.
5. Ibid, Vol. I p.216.
6. Ibid, Vol. II pp.118-119.

Snowshill from Tudor Times until 1800

1. Hockaday Abstracts, Gloucester Public Library.
2. Men and Armour for Gloucestershire in 1608, ed. J. Smith, 1902.
3. E. A. B. Barnard, Stanton and Snowshill, Cambridge University Press, 1927. p.70.
4. Gloucestershire Notes and Queries, Vol. II, 1887.
5. E. A. B. Barnard, Stanton and Snowshill, pp.75-76.
6. Ibid, pp.90-91.
7. Ibid, pp.91-92.

The Nineteenth Century

1. Rev. F. E. Witts, The Diary of a Cotswold Parson, ed. David Verey, Alan Sutton, 1979, p.43 and p.123.
2. Highway Robbery Handbill — photocopy in Gloucestershire Record Office, reference D2267/Z1.
3. E. A. B. Barnard, Stanton and Snowshill, p.108.
4. T.B.G.A.S., Vol. 41, 1918-1919.
5. Gloucestershire Record Office, reference D2267/X3.
6. Ibid.

Bibliography

Manuscript Sources

Various papers in the Gloucestershire Record Office.
Various papers in the Worcestershire Record Office.
The "Hockaday Abstracts" in Gloucester Public Library.
Charles Wade's notes and other papers in the possession of the National Trust.
Papers relating to Snowshill Hill.
Text of the Mummers Play.
"The History of Snowshill" by George Cooke.

Published Books and Articles

Sir Robert Atkyns,
   The Ancient and Present State of Gloucestershire, 1712, reprint 1974.
E. A. B. Barnard,
   Stanton and Snowshill, Cambridge University Press, 1927.
Ralph Bigland,
   Historical, Monumental and Genealogical Collections Relative to the County of Gloucester, 1791-1889.
Michael Bland,
   Snowshill, Gloucestershire.
Asa Briggs,
   A Social History of England, Weidenfeld & Nicholson, 1983.
William Buchan,
   John Buchan — A Memoir, Buchan & Enright, 1982.
George Cooke,
   Snowshill in Gloucestershire, 1979.
G. R. Crosher,
   Along the Cotswold Ways, Cassell, 1976.
The Evesham Journal — various issues.
C. I. Fell,
   Shenberrow Hill Camp, Transactions B.G.A.S. 1961, Vol. 80.
H. P. R. Finberg,
   The Gloucestershire Landscape, Hodder & Stoughton, 1975.
Josceline Finberg,
   The Cotswolds, Eyre Methuen, 1977.
Gloucestershire Subsidy Roll 1327, privately printed, 1856.
William Greenwell
   Archaeologia, Recent Researches in Barrows in Yorkshire, Wiltshire, Berkshire, etc., 1889.
Charles & Alice Mary Hadfield, ed.,
   The Cotswolds — A New Study, David & Charles, 1973.
George Haigh,
   History of Winchcombe Abbey, Skeffington & Son, 1947.
C. C. Houghton,
   A Walk about Broadway, Ian Allen, 1980.
Inclosure Act for Snowshill.
Kelly's Directory 1870, 1876, 1879, 1885, 1889, 1897, 1906, 1910, 1914, 1919, 1923, 1927, 1935, 1939.
Celia Miller, ed.,
   The Account Books of Thomas Smith, Ireley Farm, Hailes, Gloucestershire, 1865-71, B.G.A.S., 1985.
John S. Moore, translator,
   Domesday Book — Gloucestershire, Phillimore, 1982.

Helen O'Neil,
 Bevan's Quarry Round Barrow, Temple Guiting, Gloucestershire, 1964, Transactions
 B.G.A.S., 1967, Vol. 86.
J. B. Priestley,
 English Journey, Heinemann, 1934 and 1984.
Samuel Rudder,
 A New History of Gloucestershire, 1779.
Percy C. Rushen,
 The History and Antiquities of Campden, privately printed 1899.
Gordon Russell,
 Designer's Trade, Allen & Unwin, 1975.
Anne Savage, translator,
 Anglo-Saxon Chronicle, Papermac, 1982.
Alan Savile, ed.,
 Archaeology in Gloucestershire, Cheltenham Art Gallery and Museum and B.G.A.S., 1984.
Brian Smith and Elizabeth Ralph,
 A History of Bristol and Gloucestershire, Phillimore, 2nd ed., 1982.
J. Smith, ed.,
 Men and Armour for Gloucestershire in 1608, Henry Sotheran & Co., 1902.
Christopher Taylor,
 Roads and Tracks of Britain, J. M. Dent & Son, 1979.
Christopher Taylor,
 Village and Farmstead, George Philip, 1983.
Nicholas Thomas,
 A Guide to Prehistoric England, Batsford, 1960.
Reverend F. E. Witts, ed. David Verey,
 The Diary of a Cotswold Parson, Alan Sutton, 1978.

Index

83